EFFECTIVE ALTERNATIVE EDUCATION PROGRAMS

Effective Alternative Education Programs

Best Practices from Planning through Evaluating

CHRISTOPHER SCOTT CHALKER, Ed.D.

Practitioner and Consultant
The Institute of Effective Practices in Alternative Education

TECHNOMIC
PUBLISHING CO., INC.

LANCASTER · BASEL

Effective Alternative Education Programs
aTECHNOMIC publication

Published in the Western Hemisphere by
Technomic Publishing Company, Inc.
851 New Holland Avenue, Box 3535
Lancaster, Pennsylvania 17604 U.S.A.

Distributed in the Rest of the World by
Technomic Publishing AG
Missionsstrasse 44
CH-4055 Basel, Switzerland

Printed in the United States of America
10 9 8 7 6 5 4 3 2

Main entry under title:
  Effective Alternative Education Programs:
    Best Practices from Planning through Evaluating

A Technomic Publishing Company book
Bibliography: p. 203

Library of Congress Catalog Card No. 96-60271
ISBN No. 1-56676-412-2

To my father, Dr. Donald M. Chalker:
Thanks for being a mentor, my inspiration,
and lifelong role model. You are the ultimate
father and educator all rolled into one.

To Georgia Governor Zell Miller:
Your vision as the driving force
behind the creation of the "Crossroads
Alternative School Consortium" has
made Georgia a national leader in
statewide alternative education initiatives.

Contents

On following your dreams . . .
If you have built castles in the air, your work need not be lost; that is where
they should be. Now put the foundations under them.

—*Henry David Thoreau*

Many effective alternative schools around the nation use successful practices that are virtually unknown to anyone but existing practitioners. Those who publicize effective practices in the literature often leave the reader with a conceptual picture at best. Therefore, practitioners new to the field, or existing alternative educators looking for new methods and strategies, can benefit from an organized, comprehensive description of "best practices" in the field of alternative education. This book will serve as a vehicle for providing the reader with an A-to-Z resource of best practices in alternative education from planning through evaluating.

This book evolved from an initial identification of concepts reported in the literature as effective in alternative education settings. In addition to a review of the literature, identification occurred through the personal experiences of the author as an alternative education practitioner, and through informal roundtable discussions with groups of alternative educators during conferences and workshops. Concepts were organized, named, and tested in a lab school setting, operating as a fully functioning alternative school. Practices found effective after testing were categorized via a taxonomy into several domains or classifications: *planning, development, implementation,* and *evaluation.*

This classification system is the foundation for what is referred to in this book as the "Institute of Effective Practices." An educator looking for a strategy, stage, or solution to a problem can reference a specific domain for information pertaining to the "best practice" in question. For example, a school district planning to start an alternative program can reference the taxonomy of best practices in the program planning domain. After completing the planning phase, district personnel can then move on to the development taxonomy. Another example highlights the existing alternative school. Let's say alternative school personnel are interested in evaluation after having been in operation for two years. By referencing the taxonomy of best practices in the evaluation domain, school personnel can find a listing of practices with descriptors used to evaluate alternative programs. Instruments specifically designed to evaluate alternative educators and their practices are included in the Appendices for this domain.

With the above examples in mind, public school administrators and alternative educators will find this handbook useful in planning and developing alternative programs for the at-risk students. Educational professionals at the national and state level will also find the book of value during activities aimed at school improvement initiatives. Further, government, corporate America, and community agencies interested in funding private and public educational alternatives for at-risk youth can use this handbook as a reference guide during any or all of the planning, developing, implementation, and evaluation stages. This handbook has been written in an easy-to-read style with reproducible forms and documents accessible to busy administrators and educational professionals from all walks of life.

Competing books on the market superficially discuss at-risk characteristics and programs from a research and conceptual standpoint, but fail to provide educators with the practical means to carry out the task of planning, development, implementation, and evaluation. After exposure to the concepts, research, and practices characterizing effective alternative education, therefore, readers often become motivated to make a difference in the lives of at-risk youth, but lack the skills and practical application to implement their ideas.

This handbook differs from competing volumes in several ways. First, it provides the reader with a step-by-step method for planning, developing, implementing, and evaluating the type of alternative program desired, based on local needs and available resources. Second, sample reproducible documents and forms are provided in the Appendices to reinforce concepts discussed in the text. Lastly, the book is divided into individual planning, development, implementation, and evaluation domains, making it easy for the reader to reference any one of these areas without having to read prerequisite material. For example, a school administrator who has an existing program but is interested in implementing a new curricular strategy can refer directly to curricular practices in Chapter 7, bypassing the first six chapters if desired.

For having the vision and drive to initiate a statewide alternative education program, I would like to thank Georgia Governor Zell Miller and the Crossroads Alternative Education Consortium, consisting of the Department of Human Resources (DHR), the Department of Children and Youth Services (DCYS), Georgia Cities In Schools (GCIS), the Department of Education (DOE), the Office of Planning and Budget (OPB), the Georgia Partnership for Excellence in Education (GPEE), and the Department of Medical Assistance (DMA). The members of the consortium work together to save and educate our children. As one of the original twenty-nine locally funded alternative education programs in Georgia, I can fully appreciate what your state funding and resource initiatives have done for alternative education. With well over 100 current programs operating as a result of your efforts, Georgia is truly a model for other states considering large-scale alternative education initiatives.

For having the insight and resolve to begin providing educational alternatives for its students years before it became fashionable, I would like to thank the Liberty County School System, Hinesville/Ft. Stewart, Georgia. Given the flexibility and autonomy to create an effective alternative education program through trial and error, and the discovery of "best" practices, I am in a position to share with others the fruits of my labor. Until now, students in the Liberty County School System have been the real benefactors. In the spirit of that initial insight and resolve shown by the Liberty County School System, others may now benefit from these findings.

I would like to thank all of those authors whose literary works provided me with the ideas and concepts for developing specific practices for implementation in the lab school setting. Referenced throughout this book, these individuals provided a foundation from which the "Institute of Effective Practices" was founded.

Many alternative educators from around the United States have contributed thoughts, ideas, and concepts to this cause in a most indirect fashion. The many informal networking initiatives, roundtable discussions, and brainstorming sessions that alternative educators seem to thrive on have been invaluable. Whether it be in a plane, train, cab, restaurant, conference room, or just in passing, I thank the many alternative educators I have come into contact with over the years. You contributed to my inspiration, vision, and will: "to go where no alternative educator has gone before."

Lastly, my undying gratitude to Tangela Madge and Susan Foltyn for the significant role that they played in the growth and development of the L.E.A.D. Program. Since the program's conception, both have contributed to the testing of "best practices" as multispecialists in the teaching, criminal justice, and counseling fields.

Chapter 1

INTRODUCTION

> He who opens a school door, closes a prison.
>
> —*Victor Hugo*

Beck's (1991) examination of extant data showed that millions of adults qualify as functionally illiterate and that each year thousands of students leave school before graduation (p. 3). The rate of school dropout is of concern for many reasons. For example, Wehlage, Rutter, Smith, Lesko, and Fernandez (1989) found that most of these students cannot get jobs; many have difficulty with the law; many do not qualify for military service; and most are not prepared to be productive citizens. Similarly, Natriello, McDill, and Pallas (1985) found that a poorly educated person is more likely to require social welfare and institutional services and is increasingly more likely involved with the penal system because of criminal activities (p. 11). They argued, therefore, that our society can avoid the more costly problem of incarceration by developing at-risk intervention efforts such as opening alternative school programs, and by investing in the development of all youth (p. 6).

A HISTORICAL BACKGROUND

According to Dearman and Plisko (1979), about 25% of eighteen-year-old students in the United States do not finish high school. This rate has remained stable over the last two decades. Unless we make changes in the way we educate our youth, this rate is expected to increase in the future (Natriello et al., 1985, p. 11.) Further, the number of students who finish twelve years of school but do not receive a regular high school diploma, as well as students who fail at least one year during high school, amount to 40% of the student population. In any case, says Beck, the cost of leaving school prematurely is considerable in terms of unemployment, underemployment, crime, and incarceration (p. 4).

With widespread calls for reform of our educational system, Natriello et al. (1985) suggested:

> Education has returned to the front of policy discussions at the state and national levels. The national commission reports that generated the latest wave of school reform and the responses of policy makers tend to ignore the dropout problem in considering ways to improve education. Recommendations to raise standards for time spent in school, content of the curriculum, and amount of homework may further compound some student problems and contribute even more to the dropout problem. Potential dropouts, typically students with limited ability along the academic dimension, may have to face repeated failure with little opportunity to engage in other school activities that might afford them some sense of success. (pp. 11–13)

According to the National Assessment of Educational Progress (1985), almost a quarter of all seventeen-year-old students cannot read simple magazines. Since approximately 14% of students drop out by age seventeen, the problem becomes enormous (Slavin, Karweit, & Madden, 1989, p. 3). Orr (1987) stated that "Poor academic performance includes many personal and social pressures that have long been known to affect educational achievement and school completion in a negative way" (p. 6). More specifically, Peng (1983) identified family-related problems such as divorce, getting married, being pregnant, needing to work; and personal problems such as being sick, responding to peer pressure, becoming violent, and lacking self-esteem as reasons for poor achievement and premature school departure (p. 6).

A meta-analysis of extant research by Frymier (1989) identified forty-five factors that contribute to students being at-risk (p. 36). Of these, only retention is the direct result of low achievement in school. Retention, in turn, increases the probability of dropping out of school. Holmes and Matthews (1984) found that retention practices continue despite research showing that the potential for negative effects consistently outweighs positive outcomes. Their study concluded that proponents of retention plans should have to show the pedagogical logic behind their policies in light of the discouraging empirical evidence (p. 232).

REVIEW OF THE LITERATURE ON AT-RISK STUDENTS

What does it mean when a young person is at-risk? Sagor (1993) reported that "The term 'at-risk' has entered the educational vernacular with a vengeance. It seems that every time it is invoked it refers to a different sub-category of student. Having multiple definitions for 'at-risk' will make maintaining focus and understanding problematic" (p. 3). Ogden and Germinario (1988) believed that "All children are occasionally students-at-risk. However, there is a segment of every school population that consistently shows a lack of the intellectual, emotional, and social skills necessary to take full advantage of the educational opportunities available to them" (p. xvii). This dysfunctional segment of the student population typically has educational deficiencies and needs due to poor basic skills attainment, learning problems, low grades, disciplinary problems, and high absenteeism. These students may have been referred to a student support team or assigned to special education, a remedial program, or an alternative education program as a result of their deficiencies.

During the late 1980s, educators began to use the term "at-risk" to describe certain categories of students. The 1989 Phi Delta Kappa study of students at risk began with the assumption that "Children are at risk if they are likely to fail either in school or in life" (Frymier & Gansneder, 1989, p. 142). Lehr and Harris (1988) explained that a review of the literature does not show a formally accepted definition of the at-risk student (p. 9), but they later define the at-risk student as "One who is not working up to potential" (p. 11). The term "at-risk" seems to encompass many groups of students who have characteristics or needs that require additional learning alternatives due to retention in grade, expulsion from school, dropping out of school, or other factors.

Despite the efforts of alternative education programs, "Potential at-risk students have been ignored in the planning and intervention efforts of educators. Hence, the gap has widened between at-risk students and their higher-achieving peers" (Lehr & Harris, 1988, p. 7). Furthermore, demographic data show growth in the population of students facing school failure, expulsion, or high dropout potential. Complicated economic and social forces exacerbate problems experienced by these students. This results in increased special learning needs and calls for more structured remediation through alternative programs.

According to Slavin et al. (1989), "Students who are at risk are those who, on the basis of identified characteristics or needs, are unlikely to graduate or leave school with the basic skills because of school failure" (p. 5). One purpose served by the at-risk label is identification of categories of persons who are at-risk. Thus, the study of at-risk children may enable us to identify and intervene in student behavior that leads to failure in school before retention, expulsion, or school dropout occurs (Richardson, Casanova, Placier, & Guilfoyle, 1989, p. 4). The concern for at-risk children today reflects our nation's reawakening to the causes and consequences of grade retention, school expulsion, and dropout within society (Pellicano, 1987, p. 47). Pellicano concludes:

> It has become fashionable to identify at-risk children in terms of poverty, alcohol and drug consumption, sexual activity, school attendance, educational failure, and race and ethnicity. The causes of the condition include the breakdown of the family; the unwillingness or inability of the government and schools to meet their responsibilities to children; the permissiveness of society's value system; or the absence of values in the home or school. (p. 47)

Research by Richardson et al. (1989) showed that at-risk intervention includes identification of students who, as teenagers, begin to exhibit characteristics leading to school failure. These authors found that many educational responses to at-risk students are based on identification of these children through school-related behaviors such as low grades, suspensions, and absenteeism. Students' personal and social circumstances often cause such behavior. Thus, student problems are seen as manifestations or symptoms of psychosocial problems they bring to school (p. 5).

REVIEW OF THE LITERATURE ON
ALTERNATIVE EDUCATION

According to Morley (1991), "Alternative education is a perspective, not a procedure or program. It is based upon the belief that there are many ways to become educated, as well as many types of environments and structures within which this may occur" (p. 8). Alternative education is represented by both public and private schools, programs within these schools, and a set of strategies, beliefs, and support services that facilitate growth in academic, personal/social, and career development initiatives (p. 9). Bucci and Reitzammer (1992) found that positive attitudes on the part of all teachers, parents, students, and community members contribute to the supportive school climate that is essential for effective alternative programs (p. 66).

According to Morley (1991), alternative education means recognizing that everyone does not learn in the same way and, therefore, should be taught differently using an innovative curriculum. It means accepting that all schools do not have to be alike with the same learning environments. Therefore, it is a means of instituting variety and choice within school systems. Figure 1.1 depicts Morley's perspective of alternative education.

Bucci and Reitzammer (1992) found alternative programs to be worthwhile for at-risk students at the secondary level: "Since the traditional classroom is not always the best learning environment for at-risk students, they often benefit from alternative programs that provide opportunities to learn in other settings" (p. 65).

"While no large-scale study of alternative school programs for youth exists, there is some evidence of their effectiveness" (Orr, 1987, p. 15). Finding that most studies of alternative school programs are limited to discussions of individual programs or identification of program characteristics, Orr concluded that implementation recommendations most often include the following:

ALTERNATIVE EDUCATION is a means of ensuring that every young person may find a path to the educational goals of the community.

ALTERNATIVE EDUCATION is a means of accommodating our cultural pluralism, making available a multitude of options.

ALTERNATIVE EDUCATION is a means of providing choices to enable each person to succeed and be productive.

ALTERNATIVE EDUCATION is a means of recognizing the strengths and values of each individual by seeking and providing the best available options for all students.

ALTERNATIVE EDUCATION is a sign of excellence in any public school system and community.

ALTERNATIVE EDUCATION is a means for addressing the transformation of our schools.

Figure 1.1 *Alternative education [adapted with permission from Morley (1991), a publication of the National Dropout Prevention Network].*

That the program be small; that it be in a nontraditional setting; that it foster a close working relationship between staff and students, emphasizing support and encouragement; that it employ a comprehensive and multifaceted service approach; that it emphasize improvement of basic skills and self-esteem; and that work experience or other types of experiential learning be included. (p. 15)

DEFINING ALTERNATIVE EDUCATION

> It appears as though an alternative school is whatever the provider wants it to be, depending on the varied needs of the students in a given school district.

The previous review of the literature does not provide a formally accepted definition of an at-risk student, nor is there a commonly accepted definition for alternative education. Instead, the term *at-risk* encompasses many groups of dysfunctional students who display characteristics or needs that require alternative schooling due to academic retention in grade, disciplinary expulsion, or premature school departure, or who are identified for dropping out. Thus, it appears as though an alternative school is whatever the provider wants it to be, depending on the varied needs of the students in a given school district, making it difficult to define and describe alternative education comprehensively. In addition, Bucci and Reitzammer (1992) reported that alternative programs are often the neglected stepchildren of school districts, a fact often reinforced by community disassociation and generally negative perceptions.

Despite the difficulty in defining alternative education, some educational researchers and practitioners have described the general characteristics of different alternative school programs. For example, Hefner-Packer (1991) described alternative education as an "educational program or school designed to provide learning experiences that meet student needs in a positive environment using strategies that may be more structured or less structured than traditional educational programs" (p. 3). Beck (1991) stated that "Alternative academic and vocational programs . . . help schools meet the needs of students who have

delinquent behavior, who have withdrawn from school, who lack fundamental basic skills, and/or those for whom the regular curriculum is
boring or inappropriate" (p. 49). Beck identified special courses or
programs, schools-within-a-school, or separate schools as viable alternatives featuring individualized instruction, a key to the success of these
programs. While many practitioners provide descriptions of their programs, definitions remain varied and inconsistent.

REFERENCES

Beck, M. S. 1991. "Increasing school completion: Strategies that work," *Monographs in
Education, Vol. 13*, C. T. Holmes (Ed.). Athens, GA: College of Education,
University of Georgia.

Bucci, J. A., & Reitzammer, A. F. 1992. "Teachers make the critical difference in
dropout prevention," *The Educational Forum* , 57:63–69.

Correct Quotes. 1991. Novato, CA: Wordstar International Incorporated.

Dearman, N. B., & Plisko, V. W. 1979. *The Condition of Education* (Publication No.
ADM 82-921). Washington, DC: U.S. Government Printing Office.

Frymier, J. 1989. *A Study of Students At Risk: Collaborating to Do Research.* Bloomington, IN: Phi Delta Kappa Educational Foundation.

Frymier, J., & Gansneder, B. 1989. "The Phi Delta Kappa study of students at risk,"*Phi
Delta Kappan* , 71:142–146.

Hefner-Packer, R. 1991. "Alternative education programs: A prescription for success,"
Monographs in Education,Vol.12, C. T. Holmes (Ed.). Athens, GA: College of
Education, University of Georgia.

Holmes, C. T., & Matthews, K. M. 1984. "The effects of nonpromotion on elementary
and junior high school pupils: A meta-analysis," *Review of Educational Research,*
54(2):225–236.

Lehr, J. B., & Harris, H. W. 1988. *At-Risk, Low Achieving Students in the Classroom,*
1st ed. Washington, DC: National Education Association.

Morley, R. E. 1991. *Alternative Education.* Clemson, SC: Clemson University, National
Dropout Prevention Center.

National Assessment of Educational Progress. 1985. "The reading report card: Progress
toward excellence in our schools; trends in reading over four national assessments
1971–1984." Princeton, NJ: National Assessment of Educational Progress.

Natriello, G., McDill, E. L., & Pallas, A. M. 1985. "School reform and potential
dropouts," *Educational Leadership,* 43(1):11–13.

Ogden, E. H., & Germinario, V. 1988. *The At-Risk Student: Answers for Educators.*
Lancaster, PA: Technomic Publishing Company, Inc.

Orr, T. M. 1987. *Keeping Students in School.* San Francisco, CA: Jossey-Bass Publishers.

Pellicano, R. R. 1987. "At-risk: A view of social advantage," *Educational Leadership,*
44(6):47–49.

Peng, S. 1983. *High School Dropouts: Descriptive Information from High School and Beyond.* Washington, DC: National Center for Education Statistics, U.S. Department of Education.

Richardson, V., Casanova, U., Placier, P., & Guilfoyle, K. 1989. *School Children At-Risk.* New York: The Falmer Press.

Sagor, R. 1993. *At-risk Students: Reaching and Teaching Them.* New York: Watersun Publishing Company.

Slavin, R. E., Karweit, N. L., & Madden, N. A. 1989. *Effective Programs for Students at Risk.* Needham Heights, MA: Allyn & Bacon.

Wehlage, G. G., Rutter, R. A., Smith, G. A., Lesko, N., & Fernandez, R. R. 1989. *Reducing the Risk: Schools as Communities of Support.* New York: The Falmer Press.

Chapter 2

ALTERNATIVE EDUCATION PROGRAMS

He that will not apply new remedies must expect new evils.
—*Francis Bacon*

The alternative school perspective is based upon the belief that there are many ways to educate, as well as many types of environments and structures within which this may occur (Fizzell, 1990). All schools do not have to be alike. Instead, incorporating variety and choice within school systems makes it possible for students to realize the educational goals of the community in an environment designed to meet their needs (Iowa Association of Alternative Schools, 1990).

There are a variety of alternative programs, which differ in setting and the way they respond to the community's interests and the needs of students. Four commonly accepted alternative education settings are discussed in this chapter. Furthermore, three different types of alternative education programs are highlighted. Lastly, several alternative education delivery models are presented.

SETTINGS FOR ALTERNATIVE EDUCATION PROGRAMS

There are four commonly accepted settings for alternative education programs: the separate alternative school, school-within-a-school, continuation school, and alternative classroom settings.

9

The Separate Alternative School

Separate alternative schools are experiencing unprecedented growth in our nation's school systems and communities. Retired school buildings, community buildings, and custom-made structures are being infiltrated by separate alternative schools. Their isolated nature, self-contained structure, and use of innovative strategies make the separate alternative school the format of choice among many school systems. Hefner-Packer (1991) described the separate alternative school in the following manner:

> The separate alternative school is a separate, self-contained educational facility that uses a non-traditional structure or strategies to promote learning and social adjustment. Students who may benefit from a separate alternative environment include those not able to function within the traditional school setting. These may include potential dropouts, students with average or above average intelligence but who are deficient in basic skills, low achievers, and those who are chronically absent. (p. 11)

Another segment of the student population increasingly served by separate alternative schools are chronically disruptive youth. Due to the recent political push to rid our nation's classrooms of violence, weapons, drugs, and disruptive students, school districts have found it convenient to remove problem students from regular classrooms and reassign them to separate alternative schools through screening committees or disciplinary panels. Separate alternative schools have become the solution of choice due to their self-contained nature and isolation from regular school campuses.

Regardless of the type of student served, most separate alternative school programs use nontraditional, innovative curricular, instructional, and support strategies to reach their students. Such strategies and methods include individualized, competency-based instruction, curricular integration, structured environments, a basic skills emphasis, small pupil-teacher ratios, work study programs, and flexibility in scheduling, hours of operation, and grading. Furthermore, separate alternative schools use therapeutic means in a nurturing environment; individual, peer, and family counseling; paraprofessional and volunteer assistance; collaboration with community service agencies; and student recognition programs.

All methods and strategies used in separate alternative school programs are directly linked to goal attainment. The goals of separate alternative schools include elimination of academic failure; creation of a personal atmosphere; improved social, career, and academic skills; regular school reintegration; and development of self-esteem, self-discovery, and self-awareness (Hefner-Packer, 1991). Furthermore, separate alternative schools must provide students with opportunities for problem resolution, adjustment, and change. These factors must occur if family, school, and peer relations are to improve and stabilize. Only under these conditions can the ultimate goals of school completion and self-actualization be achieved.

The School-within-a-School Program

A second type of alternative education program is the school-within-a-school. According to Morley (1991), this model was developed primarily at the high school level to reduce the size and numbers of large schools into more manageable and humane units. The concept has evolved into an effective way of providing educational alternatives for students at-risk or in need of an alternative learning style. Unlike most separate alternative school programs, which are housed in facilities without adequate vocational, fine arts, and physical education programs, the school-within-a-school enjoys the advantage of access to regular school resources, electives, and special programs. By sharing facilities with the parent school, the school-within-a-school alternative program can provide students with vocational training and other elective courses not possible in separate programs.

Hefner-Packer (1991) described the school-within-a-school program as follows:

> The school-within-a-school is a semi-autonomous, non-traditional, or specialized educational program housed within a traditional school or in a separate facility that has strong organizational ties to the parent school. Students usually attend the program for a portion of the day and return to the traditional school for electives or special courses. Students who may benefit from the school-within-a-school environment include those who are poorly motivated, low achievers, underachievers, behind in graduation credits, and unable to adjust to traditional structure and teaching methods. (p. 10)

School systems choose the location of their school-within-a-school programs after careful consideration of available resources. School systems with building space can afford to house their alternative program within the confines of a regular school. Systems with limited space may have to house their alternative program in a separate facility. This arrangement requires a strong organizational tie and close partnership with the home school. Anything less categorizes the program as a separate alternative school.

Regardless of the physical setting of the school-within-a-school, strategies and methods employed by these programs include interrelated courses, individualized competency-based instruction, curricular integration, student contracting, low student-teacher ratio, team and peer teaching, school-community collaboration, and individual and group counseling. All strategies and methods are linked to goal attainment. According to Hefner-Packer (1991), the goals of school-within-a-school programs are to relieve pressure and increase personalism, improve student self-image, improve basic skills, increase student individualization, increase attendance, enhance morale, and improve human relations.

The Continuation School

The continuation school is an evening, summer, or regular school program that provides educational opportunities to individuals no longer attending a traditional school program or those in need of additional coursework. Included in this category are dropout prevention programs, dropout intervention programs, pregnant and parenting teen programs, evening and adult education programs, summer school programs, and grade acceleration programs.

Young (1990) described the continuation school as a program designed to provide a less competitive, more individualized approach to learning. Young found that continuation schools usually provide individualized plans that include support services, personal responsibility, nongraded or continuous progress, and personal/social development opportunities for students. Continuation schools have traditionally made up the majority of alternative schools.

According to Hefner-Packer (1991), the characteristics of the continuation school include:

> assistance in completion of graduation or GED requirements, individualized instruction in the basic skills, vocational instruction and work experience, and interrelated academic and work activities. Furthermore, instruction in pre- and postnatal care, year-round instruction, flexible hours, programmed texts and materials, tutorial services, counseling

services, student-designed schedules and programs, flexible attendance policies, extended day experiences, and credit for volunteerism are characteristic of the continuation school. (p. 12)

As for the two previously discussed alternative programs, the characteristics of the continuation school are linked to goal attainment. The first goal is preparation of individuals for a high school diploma or GED certificate. The second goal is instruction provided in a less competitive, less structured, more personalized atmosphere. Lastly, preparation of individuals for the world of work is linked to goal attainment (Hefner-Packer, 1991, p. 12).

The Alternative Classroom

Hefner-Packer (1991) described the alternative classroom in the following manner:

The alternative classroom is a self-contained classroom within a traditional school that varies from other programs in its educational methodology, structure, or learning emphasis. Students benefitting from an alternative classroom environment include those who are poorly motivated, underachievers, and behind in classwork or credits required for graduation or promotion. (p. 9)

The characteristics of an alternative classroom include individualization, competency-based instruction, longer instructional periods, student contracting, basic skills emphasis, career and vocational activities, counseling services, tutoring and mentoring opportunities, parental involvement, and integrated teaching. These characteristics are linked to goal attainment for students. In an alternative classroom, these goals include improved self-image, enhanced academic and social skills, accelerated grade promotion or opportunities for additional Carnegie units, and alternatives to graduation.

TYPES OF ALTERNATIVE EDUCATION PROGRAMS

Raywid (1994) identified three pure types of alternatives that individual programs model to varying degrees. Type I alternatives are considered *programs of choice,* Type II alternatives are considered *assignment programs,* and Type III alternatives are considered *referral programs.*

Choice Programs

Type I alternatives feature popular innovations that seek to make school challenging and fulfilling for all involved. These alternatives virtually always reflect organizational and administrative departures from the traditional school of thought. Type I alternatives are programs of choice and are usually popular. Sometimes they resemble magnet schools, and in some locales they constitute some or all of the options in choice systems. They are likely to reflect programmatic themes or emphasis pertaining to content or instructional strategy, or both.

Assignment Programs

Raywid (1994) defined Type II alternatives as programs to which students are assigned, usually as a final chance at schooling prior to expulsion. They include in-school suspension programs, timeout rooms, and long-term programs for the chroncially disruptive students. "They have been likened to 'soft-jails,' and they have nothing to do with options or choice" (p. 27). Type II programs usually focus on behavior modification and the reform of chronically disruptive students, with little attention paid to modifying curriculum or instruction. Some of these programs require students to complete work assigned in the regular classes from which they have been removed. Others simply focus on basic skills, emphasizing drill and practice and rote learning.

Referral Programs

Type III alternatives have been defined (Raywid, 1994) as programs designed for students who are presumed to need academic and/or social and emotional remediation and rehabilitation. Therefore, students are usually referred for services to Type III programs, which focus on remedial work and social/emotional development. After remediation and rehabilitation, students are reintegrated to the regular school environment, often back in their proper grade or at the appropriate skill level.

While Raywid (1994) found most alternative schools identifiable as one of these three types, particular programs, however, can be a mix of types as described below:

A compassionate staff, for example, may give a Type II program Type III overtones. Or a committed Type III staff may venture into programmatic innovations that mark a Type I. But even so, the genre determines an alternative school's most formative features. It determines the grounds upon which the school will be evaluated; whether student affiliation is by choice, sentence, or referral; and perhaps most fundamentally, what is assumed about school and students. Both Type II and Type III set out to fix the student on the assumption that the problems lie within the individual. But Type I assumes that difficulties may be explained by the school-student match and that by altering a school's program and environment, one can alter student response, performance, and achievement. (p. 27)

DELIVERY MODELS FOR ALTERNATIVE EDUCATION PROGRAMS

Several delivery models are used for alternative education programs. One or more of these models typically serve as individual components of alternative education programs, depending on the setting and the type of program offered. For example, a program in an alternative classroom setting serving students referred for remediation may be characterized by an academic intervention model. On the other hand, a separate alternative school serving students both of choice and by assignment may be characterized by several different delivery models as program components, such as behavior intervention, school continuation, and dropout intervention. Particular programs may take on a "generic look" by mixing characteristics from different models.

School Transition Model

According to Hahn (1987), hundreds of alternative secondary schools throughout the United States offer dropouts and potential dropouts a last opportunity to continue or resume their education. One type of separate alternative school, described by Hefner-Packer (1991), helps prepare students for a return to the regular school setting or graduation. The goals of such programs are the elimination of academic failure; improved social, career, and academic skills; and development of enhanced self-esteem and self-awareness. Bucci and Reitzammer (1992) stressed the importance of "special attention" given to at-risk students to ensure that progress made during the elementary years continues uninterrupted through the ensuing years. The transition from one school to another is an especially critical point for at-risk students.

Behavioral Intervention Model

McLaughlin and Vacha (1992) have documented the effectiveness of behavioral procedures as intervention strategies with at-risk children and youth. Within this model, educators use the basic principles of learning, institute effective and systematic procedures, state precise goals, and collect data to determine student progress. Behavioral intervention can help at-risk children gain the attending and survival skills required for school success.

The remediation of chronic disruptive behavior in the classroom with at-risk students has met with some success. Short (1988) presented three models used in alternative programs in which behavioral intervention is the focus. These models can be used independently of one another or to a lesser or greater degree in conjunction with one another.

ACADEMIC MODEL

In the academic model, discipline problems evolve from learning difficulties and the ensuing frustration felt by students who do not experience success in academic work. The model is based on the belief that student behavior will improve with growth in academic achievement (Short, 1988).

THERAPEUTIC MODEL

In the therapeutic model, student misbehavior is assumed to be the result of a particular problem that the student is experiencing. Therefore, it is believed that assisting the student in developing problem-solving skills will lead to problem resolution and development of appropriate behavior (Short, 1988).

PUNITIVE MODEL

The punitive model is based on the belief that students misbehave because they want to cause trouble. As a result, programs within this model operate on the assumption that punishment will serve to deter or eliminate misbehavior (Short, 1988).

Academic Intervention Model

Orr (1987) described an at-risk program combining targeted and general instructional and support strategies to increase the number of students who stay in school and graduate. Alternative programs for students at-risk of dropping out are combined with consideration of ways to restructure the schools to respond better to students' varied educational needs. Remedial and other pullout programs are examples of targeted strategies, whereas computer-assisted instruction and individualized instruction are examples of general classroom strategies.

Bucci and Reitzammer (1992) found that "The most significant and comprehensive factor in preventing at-risk students from dropping out of school is the maintenance of a positive instructional environment. . . . They drop out of school because they are failing to learn, not because they do not want to learn" (pp. 63–64). Bucci and Reitzammer go on to say that teachers should use instructional strategies to foster the academic development of students such as continuous progress, cooperative learning, peer tutoring, mentoring, rewards, and positive learning environments.

Vocational Intervention Model

Vocational intervention programs are described (Orr, 1987) as programs offering job-readiness preparation and vocational counseling to marginally performing students. The goal of these programs is to make school meaningful and prepare students for the world of work once they are through with their education. Support groups and part-time employment are strategies used in this type of program. McLaughlin and Vacha (1992) noted that career education is a viable way to keep at-risk students in school. Successful programs preventing dropout focus on the link between education and future earning power and the use of businesses, schools, and local educational foundations to assist students. Thus, these programs can easily be sponsored by organizations external to the school or integrated with an existing educational program.

School Continuation Model

School continuation programs help students cope with their competing responsibilities and provide a way for them to complete high school (Orr,

1987). Thus, such programs are designed for youth whose economic, family, or personal responsibilities keep them from completing school. A school-based day-center permitting teenage mothers to continue their high school coursework while their children are being taken care of is an example of this strategy. Bucci and Reitzammer (1992) cited an increase in the number of teenage pregnancies as a major contributor to school continuation programs. Thus, school systems in increasing numbers are providing services to pregnant teenagers in order to keep them in school or have them return to continue school.

Dropout Prevention Model

Bucci and Reitzammer (1992) described numerous plans and proposals addressing dropout prevention. "They vary from small alternative programs to system wide strategies; from short-term externally funded pilot projects to comprehensive long-range community plans" (p. 63). These efforts include enhancing self-esteem, developing alternative programs, monitoring absences, mentoring at-risk students, involving parents, and providing social and health services. Implementation of these programs by practitioners, especially teachers, ultimately determines their success.

Orr (1987) described a dropout prevention program provided for students who are likely to drop out because of serious academic and attendance problems. Such programs often combine an array of services in a comprehensive, multiservice approach that encourages students to remain in school. One such strategy is an acceleration program for helping students who have experienced past retentions in grade to catch up to their proper grade level.

Dropout Intervention Model

Bearden, Spencer, and Moracco (1989) reported that dropout intervention programs have evolved out of descriptive studies on the characteristics of high school dropouts. "Typical components of these programs include tutorial activities, alternative classes, counseling and advising, and work-related activities. To be more effective, the implementation of programs should include parental involvement, referral and outreach systems, staff commitment, environmental support, and systems of evaluation" (pp. 113–114).

Orr (1987) described dropout intervention programs for students who have already dropped out of school. Such programs combine multiple services to address the many problems facing young dropouts. The program focuses on helping youth to achieve basic skills and to obtain the General Education Diploma (GED), while also helping them to prepare for employment.

School-Community Partnership Model

School-community partnership programs go beyond the school system to encompass the larger community or city. As an alternative philosophy, this approach reflects the idea that the problems that cause students to drop out affect a much larger group than the dropouts themselves. As an alternative approach, this strategy is designed to stimulate interest in improving the organization of schooling and the incorporation of community services. This alternative practice draws on the resources of businesses, universities, and other social agencies.

Bucci and Reitzammer (1992) outlined the need for community intervention in school problems that stem from poor home environment, poor health, and poor nutrition. They conclude that "Students have access to community service experts at the school site who are capable of helping them solve their problems or who will refer them to other agencies" (p. 68). Bucci and Reitzammer also discussed the needs of at-risk students with respect to getting special attention from adult mentors. Often, these mentors are community volunteers or significant others who spend time and resources on students assigned to them.

REFERENCES

Bearden, L. J., Spencer, W. A., & Moracco, J. C. 1989. "A study of high school dropouts," *The School Counselor,* 37(2):111–119.

Bucci, J. A., & Reitzammer, A. F. 1992. "Teachers make the critical difference in dropout prevention," *The Educational Forum,* 57:63–69.

Fizzell, B. 1990. Personal communication via letter. Edu-Serve, Vancouver, WA.

Hahn, A. 1987. "Reaching out to America's dropouts: What to do?" *Phi Delta Kappan,* 69:256–263.

Hefner-Packer, R. 1991. "Alternative education programs: A prescription for success," *Monographs in Education, Vol. 12,* C. T. Holmes (Ed.). Athens, GA: College of Education, University of Georgia.

Iowa Association of Alternative Schools. 1990. Brochure. Available from Kathy Knudt-son, 1212 7th St. S.E., Cedar Rapids, IA 52401.

McLaughlin, T. F., & Vacha, E. F. 1992. "School programs for at-risk children and youth: A review," *Education and Treatment of Children*, 15(3):255–267.

Morley, R. E. 1991. *Alternative Education*. Clemson, SC: Clemson University, National Dropout Prevention Center.

Orr, T. M. 1987. *Keeping Students in School*. San Francisco, CA: Jossey-Bass Publishers.

Raywid, M. A. 1994. "Alternative schools: The state of the art," *Educational Leadership*, 52(1):26–30.

Short, P. M. 1988. "Planning and developing in-school suspension programs," *Monographs in Education, Vol. 9*, C. T. Holmes (Ed.). Athens, GA: College of Education, University of Georgia.

Young, T. 1990. *Public Alternative Education*. New York: Teachers College Press.

Chapter 3

BEST PRACTICES IN ALTERNATIVE EDUCATION: PLANNING THROUGH EVALUATING

He who chooses the beginning of a road chooses the place it leads to. It is the means that determine the end.

—*Harry Emerson Fosdick*

THE TAXONOMICAL CLASSIFICATION OF BEST PRACTICES

Webster's New World Dictionary (Guralnik, 1992) defines a taxonomy as "the science of classification; laws and principles covering the classifying of objects." A taxonomical classification system is the most efficient method of structuring best practices in alternative education. Since alternative education is characterized by diversity and innovation, structuring best practices in different categories helps the reader get an overview of the multitude of information in this rapidly growing field.

Best practices in alternative education is classified using several different domains. *Webster's New World Dictionary* defines a domain as "a field or sphere of activity or influence." Classifying best practices by domain simplifies an understanding of the material and allows readers to access practices of interest to them by referencing the domain in question.

IDENTIFICATION OF THE TAXONOMICAL DOMAINS

As displayed in Figure 3.1, the domains presented in this book are categorized as planning, development, implementation, and evaluation.

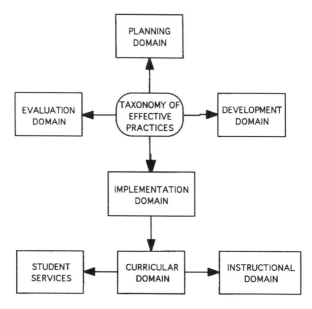

Figure 3.1 The taxonomical domains.

The implementation domain consists of three subcategories: curricular practices, instructional practices, and student services.

A DESCRIPTIVE OVERVIEW OF THE DOMAINS

Figure 3.2 charts best practices sequentially in each of the taxonomical domains. Best practices in each domain represent as a whole the purpose of that particular domain.

Best practices in the planning domain constitute the initial stage in the process of constructing alternative education programs. Planning practices lay the groundwork from which to build, followed by development of collaboratives, resources, and funding proposals as the second stage in the process. These development practices provide a framework for the planning foundation. After planning and development practices have resulted in a finished structure, program implementation occurs. Implementation of curricular practices, instructional practices, and student services provides the furnishings and operational aspects of the structure. These are the so-called "guts" of the program. Lastly, the evaluation

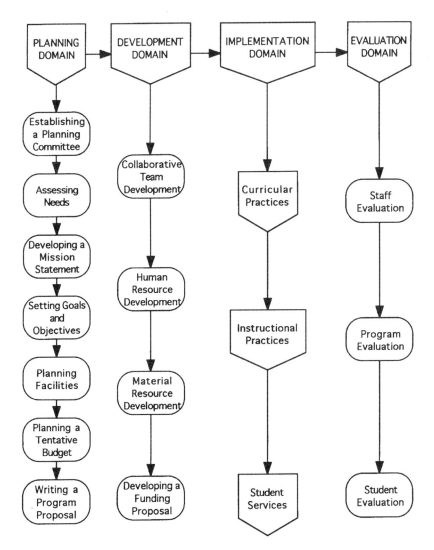

Figure 3.2 *Best practices.*

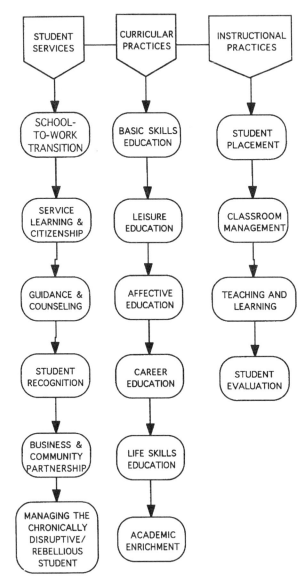

Figure 3.2 (continued) *Best practices.*

domain contains methods for assessing the newly constructed program and its occupants, students and staff members.

IDENTIFICATION OF BEST PRACTICES IN THE VARIOUS DOMAINS

The previous section provided an overview of the purpose of each taxonomical domain. Best practices are sequentially organized under their respective domain in Figure 3.2. Each has a specific purpose in the overall creation of alternative education programs. Individuals following the practices in each domain in the order in which they fall will find that the process of program creation is fairly straightforward. Similarly, individuals isolating particular practices for their singular use in existing programs will find the process very "user friendly" and efficient.

Following is a discussion of best practices in each taxonomical domain.

The Planning Domain

The planning domain contains seven separate practices that are sequentially related: establishing a planning committee, assessing needs, developing a mission statement, setting goals and objectives, planning facilities, planning a budget, and writing a proposal for program approval.

Establishing a planning committee is an important first step in the planning process, as the planning committee should be actively involved and oversee the six remaining steps in the process. Assessment of needs, however, is where it all begins! Assessing school and community needs lays a framework from which to build. Thus, an efficient alternative education program is one whose programs are based on a blueprint of school/community needs. Programs can be constructed to serve both students in alternative placement by assignment and those in alternative placement by choice, depending on the needs of the school/community.

From the needs assessment surface the mission statement and goals and objectives. These are set in motion by the planning committee after analysis of the needs assessment data. From the program goals and objectives comes a clearer picture of facility needs and the framework for a tentative budget. A proposal for program approval should be the end result of work in each of the above areas. This proposal will ultimately be reviewed by the local board of education.

The Development Domain

The development domain contains four separate practices that are sequentially related: collaborative team development, human resource development, material resource development, and developing funding proposals.

The first step in this domain is to develop an ongoing collaborative team from the initial planning committee. After the necessary adjustments in membership, the collaborative team becomes actively involved in the process of developing human resources, material resources, and funding proposals. The collaborative team continues to oversee and govern the program through the implementation and evaluation phases, as well as in the future.

The Implementation Domain

The implementation domain consists of three practices: curricular, instructional, and student services. Curricular practices include basic skill education, leisure education, affective education, career education, life skills education, and academic enrichment. Instructional practices include student placement, classroom management, teaching and learning, and student evaluation. Student services include school-to-work transition, service learning and citizenship, guidance and counseling, student recognition, business and community partnerships, and managing the chronically disruptive/rebellious student. These practices will be broken down further in the text to illustrate their specific use in creating alternative education programs.

The Evaluation Domain

The evaluation domain consists of three separate, but equally important practices: program evaluation, student evaluation, and staff evaluation. Program evaluation often involves using the collaborative team, students, parents, and staff members as evaluators. Student evaluation is usually completed by staff members and through self-evaluation. Staff evaluation is typically completed by administrators, through self-evaluation, or by peer evaluators.

REFERENCE

Guralnik, D. B. 1992. *Webster's New World Dictionary of the American Language,* 2nd ed. New York: Simon and Schuster, Publishers.

THE PLANNING DOMAIN

> It does not take much strength to do things, but it requires great strength to decide on what to do.
>
> —*Elbert Hubbard*

Chapter 4 suggests an agenda for planning committee members when planning alternative education programs. The agenda is not written in stone, however, as it may require modifications based on local school, home, and community needs identified during the initial assessment phase. Thereafter, developing a mission statement from the needs assessment, setting goals and objectives, planning facilities, and planning a tentative budget are all suggested steps in the planning domain. The planning committee's agenda leads to a program proposal submitted to the local board of education for approval (Figure 4.1).

Planning requires that activities related to the development, implementation, and evaluation domains be addressed when setting goals and objectives. Development activities involve developing a collaborative team, human and material resources, and a funding proposal. Implementation activities include implementing curricular practices, instructional practices, and student services. Evaluation activities involve evaluating staff members, programs, and students.

Appendices A through F contain sample forms for use in planning alternative education programs. They include: choosing a planning committee, conducting various needs assessments, developing a mission

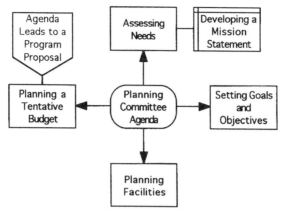

Figure 4.1 The planning domain.

statement, developing goals and objectives, choosing facilities, and planning a budget.

THE PRACTICE OF ESTABLISHING
A PLANNING COMMITTEE

The planning committee consists of educators from all grade levels, parents, students, and community representatives. With a few adjustments, the planning committee can be transformed into an ongoing collaborative to oversee the total alternative program during the development, implementation, and evaluation domains.

A planning committee comprised of individuals committed to the improvement of education provides consistency, not only in program planning, but also in program development, implementation, and evaluation. Hefner-Packer (1991) found that committees function best if membership is not less than six and no more than fifteen. Committee members must be representative of the school, community, and family, including a classroom teacher and administrator from each grade level, an auxiliary staff member, business representative, social service representative, senior citizen, student, and parent.

Appendix A provides reproducible worksheet I for use in choosing planning committee members.

As part of a strategic plan for operation, the planning committee must conduct an assessment of needs, develop a mission statement, establish goals and objectives, plan a tentative budget, and plan for facilities. In order to complete this process, goals and objectives must also address the development, implementation, and evaluation domains described in later chapters.

Hefner-Packer (1991) advised that committee members be informed of their responsibilities and time commitment in relation to planning an effective alternative education program. The work of the planning committee should result in a written alternative program proposal for submission to the superintendent and board of education for review and approval.

THE PRACTICE OF ASSESSING NEEDS

> Developing program components based on local needs, identified through a formal needs assessment using a variety of stakeholders, is an effective practice in alternative education.

The purpose of a needs assessment is to develop priorities and goals for the creation of alternative education programs based on current and specific problem areas. The continuing emphasis on accountability and effectiveness has encouraged leaders to assess needs on a periodic basis. Needs assessments are enhancements of the self-study approach. They provide a valuable strategy for examining the state of community, home, and school affairs (Swan, 1990).

Kaufman (1972) described a needs assessment as a formal process that determines the gaps between current outputs or outcomes and required or desired outcomes or inputs; places these gaps in priority order; and selects the most important for resolution (Hefner-Packer, 1991, p. 33). Kaufman (1972) characterized a needs assessment in the following manner:

The data must represent the actual world of learners and related people, both as it exists now and as it will, could, and should exist in the future.

No needs determination is final and complete; we must realize that any statement of needs is in fact tentative, and we should constantly question the validity of our needs statements. Any discrepancies should be identified in terms of products or actual behaviors, not in terms of processes. (p. 29)

The planning committee is responsible for ensuring that a needs assessment is conducted. In addition to demographic data depicting the state of community, family, and school affairs, input from members of the school system, business and community sector, and social service agencies is sought as part of the needs assessment (Figure 4.2). During needs assessment, the activities of the planning committee should include a discussion of a manageable number of issues and concerns leading to a mission statement. Data on both issues and concerns should be reviewed as a means of defining the mission statement. The planning committee must analyze the data to determine existing conditions requiring attention.

Appendix B contains reproducible worksheets II–V for implementing a comprehensive needs assessment.

THE PRACTICE OF DEVELOPING A MISSION STATEMENT

Barry (1986) defined an organization's mission as a statement of its basic purpose or reason for existence. The mission describes what is to

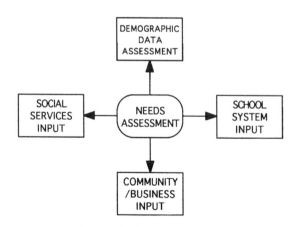

Figure 4.2 The needs assessment.

be accomplished in the long run and with whom. For example, Barry suggested a possible mission of a prenatal health program might be "to reduce infant mortality for low-income families."

Clarity about your organization's basic mission is critical to effective strategic planning. It is very difficult to chart a course for the future when you are unclear about your mission. A poor mission is one that lacks direction. As a result, programs become ends in themselves, with little thought of the ultimate outcome or impact desired.

A good strategic plan clearly states an organization's mission and how it is to be accomplished. This includes what facilities, services, staff, funding, and material resources are most likely to produce the results you desire (Barry, 1986). An effective mission statement is one which is general enough to be everlasting but specific enough to have a precise direction.

Appendix C contains reproducible worksheet VI for use in developing a mission statement.

THE PRACTICE OF SETTING GOALS AND OBJECTIVES

> The planning committee must use needs assessment data as a basis for formulating alternative education program goals and objectives.

Hefner-Packer (1991) described a goal as the vision and objectives as the outcomes for alternative education programs. Since objectives facilitate the process of accomplishing goals, both goals and objectives address the intent of the alternative education program as shown in Figure 4.3.

Appendix D contains reproducible worksheet VII for use in developing program goals and objectives.

Intent of the alternative education program is reflected in the nature of the objectives and whom the objectives affect. How much the planning committee expects to accomplish, and when, is critical to the overall success of the program. Stating objectives specifically and in measurable terms will lead to effective program development, implementation, and evaluation. How a particular objective is to be accomplished will set the stage for subsequent domains.

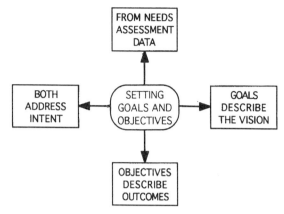

Figure 4.3 Goals and objectives.

THE PRACTICE OF PLANNING FACILITIES

Renovating a vacant, retired school building and using services and resources provided by an existing partner school is a cost-effective practice in alternative education.

A critical aspect of the planning domain is facilities planning. Planning facilities entails using one of five approaches, depending on the individual school system's situation. For example, the planning committee can use existing operational school buildings, existing community/business buildings, retired school buildings, retired community/business buildings, or a custom-made facility built to program specifications.

Any of the above designs can make use of an existing partner school providing resources and services to the alternative school facility. This cost-efficient method of operation calls on the partner school to provide counseling services, repositioned staff, media center resources, vocational education, food service, and transportation to the alternative school. This approach limits direct costs to new building construction, existing facilities renovation, and/or the purchase price of facilities outside of the school system.

Appendix E contains reproducible worksheet VIII for use in planning facilities.

Existing Operational School Building

The most cost-efficient method of providing facilities for an alternative school is to share an existing school building with the regular program. This can be accomplished either by using a classroom or wing during regular school hours, or by using the facilities during evening hours as a school continuation program. Each method of sharing provides easy access to the resources and services afforded the regular school population.

Existing Community/Business Buildings

Unless space is donated in an existing community or business building, this facilities arrangement can be the most costly of the methods listed previously. Renting or leasing building space is not very cost-efficient for this type of endeavor. Instead, partnerships with community agencies or businesses, including donated building space, is the most cost-efficient of the methods.

Retired School Buildings

Those systems wanting a truly separate alternative school, but desiring a cost-efficient method of accomplishing this, may be able to utilize an old, retired school building if one exists in their district. Most frequently, retired elementary school buildings are used. In Georgia, for example, the latest state to implement a statewide alternative education initiative, 75% of the alternative schools are based in retired elementary schools (Chalker, 1994). These buildings can be renovated to the specifications of the particular alternative education program. Innovations such as converting a classroom into a weight training room and utilizing a regular school partner for resources and services can compensate for the lack of facilities such as a gymnasium or media center as shown in Figure 4.4.

Retired Community/Business Buildings

Unless donated or provided through a partnership arrangement, a retired community or business building can be costly. Purchasing a building for use as an alternative school is not the most cost-efficient of the measures, to say the least. Unless this is the only avenue available to

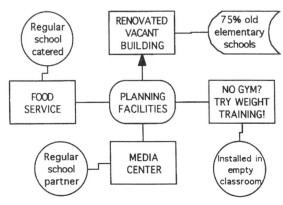

Figure 4.4 *Facilities planning.*

a school district, it may be wise to consider finding a partner or an adopt-a-school sponsor to offset the costs involved.

Custom-Made Facility Built to Specifications

School systems that are in a position to finance building construction should consider a custom-made facility when planning their alternative school program. The facility can be located on an existing school campus or on other property belonging to the school system. The facility should be designed with the assessed needs and goals and objectives of the program in mind. Long-term goals must be considered when designing the facility to meet future expansion needs.

THE PRACTICE OF PLANNING A TENTATIVE BUDGET

> Seeking out grant funds, sponsorships, and cost-free components as alternatives to school system funding is an effective practice in planning an alternative education budget.

A tentative first-year operating budget should itemize proposed expenditures and funding sources, including local, public, and private funds

(Figure 4.5). The budget should also reflect entities that were one-time expenses and require no additional expenditure of funds, such as furniture, equipment, and materials. Another popular funding method requires regular school campuses to share resources with the alternative school. Expenditures of this type incur only an indirect cost to the school system with regard to the alternative education budget. Additionally, corporate or business sponsorships should be recognized for their positive impact on required budget amounts.

The first-year budget should be part of a local plan that demonstrates a long-term commitment to alternative education. Consider such related costs as transportation, food service, facilities, and set-up costs. Local providers should make every attempt to obtain public and private funds, and to commit local funds to proposed programs. The cost-effectiveness of the proposed program is critical to acceptance of the budget.

Using innovative, cost-effective strategies to implement the alternative education program minimizes budget needs. So-called "cost-free" strategies is an even more effective way to provide services when under tight budget constraints. For example, assigning alternative school students to a local elementary school as teacher assistants in a service learning program for elective credit costs absolutely nothing. Using students as resources in their own program of learning is another "freebie." The returns always exceed the initial investment.

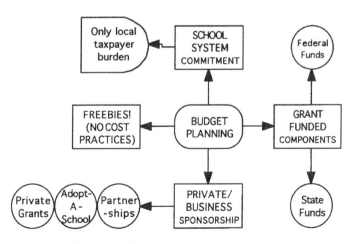

Figure 4.5 *The practice of planning a budget.*

> Using volunteers, guest presenters, school sponsors, work study sponsors, and partner schools for the purpose of providing services and internship experiences for students are effective practices in cost-effective budget planning. Using partner schools is the best way to keep from duplicating services when working with a limited budget.

"When building a budget for an alternative education program, an effective planning tool is to determine and enter proposed expenditures and revenues on a spreadsheet" (Hefner-Packer, 1991, p. 73). Such a spreadsheet is included in Appendix A. Listed expenses on one side of the spreadsheet include salaries, benefits, instructional supplies, office supplies, custodial services, facilities, furniture, technology, equipment, etc. Expenditures include those related, as well as indirect costs incurred as part of the program. Revenues itemized on the adjacent side of the spreadsheet include local funds, public funds, private funds, sponsorship funds, and resources donated.

Appendix F contains reproducible worksheet IX for use in program budget planning.

THE PRACTICE OF WRITING A PROPOSAL FOR PROGRAM APPROVAL

> Using needs assessment data, goal setting, and facilities and budget planning to construct a custom-made program proposal is an effective practice in alternative education.

At the conclusion of the planning phase, a proposal, the "grand finale," must be developed and submitted by the planning committee to the superintendent and board of education for review and acceptance. Key staff members, community leaders, parents, and students not assigned to the planning committee should have the opportunity to review and respond to the proposal prior to submission. Sufficient time for review and revision of the proposal must be provided.

The planning committee should ensure that the necessary information is included in the program proposal: an abstract of the program; the needs assessment data; the goals, objectives, and activities pertaining to the development, implementation, and evaluation domains; the facilities study; and the tentative budget. Contents of the program proposal abstract, adapted from Hefner-Packer (1991), include:

- an explanation of why and in what manner the program is an alternative to regular education
- a description of the assessed need, target population, and methodology for program development, implementation, and evaluation
- a discussion of how courses of instruction and days of actual student attendance will be affected
- a recommended length of time for program trial and evaluation of effectiveness
- a review of local and state department of education requirements, standards, guidelines, and funding sources for alternative education programs (p. 36)

REFERENCES

Barry, B. W. 1986. *Strategic Planning Workbook for Nonprofit Organizations.* St. Paul, MN: Amherst H. Wilder Foundation.

Chalker, C. S. 1994. A Description of Separate Secondary Alternative School Programs in Georgia in 1993–94. Unpublished doctoral dissertation, The University of Georgia, Athens, GA.

Hefner-Packer, R. 1991. "Alternative education programs: A prescription for success," *Monographs in Education, Vol. 12,* C. T. Holmes (Ed.). Athens, GA: College of Education, University of Georgia.

Kaufman, R. A. 1972. *Educational System Planning.* Englewood Cliffs, NJ: Educational Technology Publications, Inc.

Swan, W. W. 1990. "Needs assessments for special programs," *Monographs in Education, Vol. 11,* C. T. Holmes (Ed.). Athens, GA: College of Education, University of Georgia.

Chapter 5

THE DEVELOPMENT DOMAIN

> We have a choice: to plow new ground or let the weeds grow.
> —*Jonathan Westover*

The development domain begins with three separate but sequential practices as shown in Figure 5.1. *Collaborative team development, material resource development,* and *human resource development* are all prerequisites to the development of a funding proposal, the fourth practice in the domain. The smart school official puts together a comprehensive collaborative team to address both human and material resource development before submitting funding proposals for program operation.

FROM PLANNING COMMITTEE TO COLLABORATIVE TEAM

Developing a collaborative team whose members consist of a variety of community, business, family, and school representatives is an effective practice in program development.

The collaborative team consists of a variety of members as charted in Figure 5.2. With a few adjustments in membership, the planning com-

41

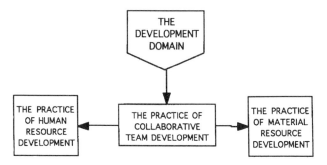

Figure 5.1 *The development domain.*

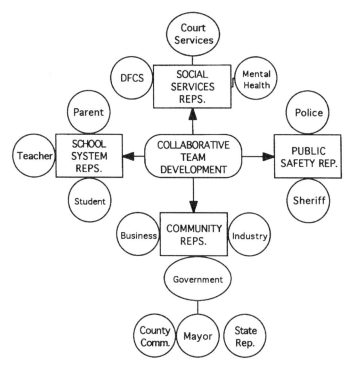

Figure 5.2 *Collaborative team development.*

mittee discussed in the planning domain can easily be transformed into a collaborative team during program development. Some members of the short-term planning committee may not be considered for a long-term position as a collaborative team member. On the other hand, new positions may be added. In any case, the team should consist of those stakeholders impacted in some way by the alternative program who can make a contribution to its operation and enhancement.

The collaborative team is used to oversee the development, implementation, and evaluation phases of operation. Members also act in an advisory and support capacity for the alternative education program. Collaborative teams are necessary prerequisites when writing funding proposals and receiving grant funds.

Social Service Representatives

Social service representatives are valuable assets to the collaborative team due to the multitude of services they offer to children and youth. Additionally, social service agencies such as Juvenile Court Services, Department of Family and Children Services (DFCS) and Mental Health usually have a number of clients enrolled in alternative education programs. These factors qualify social service agencies as stakeholders in local efforts to provide alternative education programs and warrant their placement on a collaborative team.

Public Safety Representatives

Public safety representatives are also valuable assets to the collaborative team due to their service in the community, experience, and commitment to juvenile delinquency prevention. Policemen and sheriff deputies often act as mentors, guest speakers, and presenters in alternative education programs. For these reasons, public safety representatives qualify as stakeholders in local efforts to provide alternative education programs and warrant their inclusion on a collaborative team.

Community Representatives

Community representatives are another valuable group for the collaborative team to tap into due to their link to local government, politics, business, and industry. Public officials such as county commissioners, mayors, and state representatives often provide support for funding, make contributions to special programs, and provide jobs for work study programs. These factors qualify community representatives as stakeholders in local efforts to provide alternative education programs and warrant their placement on a collaborative team.

School System Representatives

School system representatives are also valuable to the collaborative team due to their direct involvement with alternative education programs. Teachers, students, and parents often provide important feedback about programs, have a personal stake in alternative education, and are loyal program supporters. Additionally, positive public relations require the involvement of these stakeholders in the day-to-day operation of alternative programs and warrant their placement on a collaborative team.

STAFF AND HUMAN RESOURCE DEVELOPMENT

> Using grant-funded staff, volunteers, and repositioned staff from regular schools and social service agencies instead of a total local commitment is an effective practice in alternative education.

Most school systems are not in a position to pay for alternative education programs using a total local commitment. Developing human resources for these programs usually requires grant-funded staff members, volunteers, and repositioned staff members as charted in Figure 5.3.

Locally Funded Staff

Securing local school system funding for alternative education program staffing is often difficult, to say the least. Thus, alternative education programs that can boast of local funding are rare. Local board of education members, fearing an additional taxpayer burden, often require

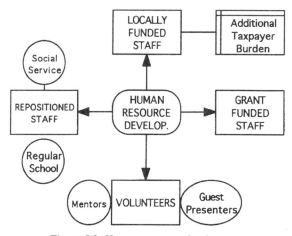

Figure 5.3 *Human resource development.*

other means of funding for proposed alternative education programs. Even school systems that are not financially strapped have to pinch pennies to make ends meet. Most school systems welcome outside sources of funding for staffing their alternative education programs.

Grant-Funded Staff

School systems often look to grants as sources of funding for staffing alternative education programs. Many grants are rewarded with few or no matching funds required by the local school system. Local school systems that successfully land grants enhance their programs with a minimum of risk financially. The only risk of grant funds is the prospect that they will some day be retired, leaving the school system with the task of finding other funding sources. Nonetheless, grant funds are worthwhile for aspiring alternative education programs looking for ways to fund their particular staffing needs.

Use of Volunteers

Volunteers are every alternative educator's dream. Individuals volunteering their services on the campus, in the classroom, or with individual students provide an additional human resource that costs nothing. Volunteers enhance the ability of alternative education programs to provide services to students, causing pupil-staff ratios to decrease. Volunteers may serve as mentors, tutors, guest presenters, lecturers, and training facilitators.

MENTORS

Volunteers used as mentors for individual students is a rapidly growing practice. Citizens, business representatives, government officials, and community service representatives can be matched with individual students for the purpose of assisting them with their schooling, personal and social development, and goal attainment. Mentors have also been known to do special things for their students, such as luncheons, gifts, and awards. Mentors have had a very positive effect on students at-risk, especially in terms of self-esteem.

GUEST PRESENTERS

Volunteers acting as guest presenters for alternative education classes or assemblies have been found to be effective for several reasons. First, diversity in planning has resulted in guest presenters serving programs in several different capacities, as speaker, lecturer, and training facilitator. Second, guest presenters offer students a different learning approach than usual. Lastly, teachers are afforded a sometimes rare break for planning, recordkeeping, or simply a breather.

The use of volunteers is what this author calls a "freebie" in the world of alternative education financing. With this practice of human resource development, alternative education programs cannot go wrong. If still in doubt, consider that volunteerism is an honorable and rewarding endeavor for those involved. As a result, volunteerism is a no-lose situation for alternative educators and volunteers alike.

Repositioned Staff

In these times of belt tightening and penny pinching by local boards of education, the concept of repositioning staff members from social service agencies and regular schools is a blessing in disguise. Repositioning is both cost-efficient and effective. The concept requires local social service agencies and/or boards of education to reposition staff members to alternative education programs either full- or part-time. Using existing staff members for repositioning requires no additional direct expenditures. It is an indirect expense, the most cost-efficient means of providing resources.

REPOSITIONED STAFF FROM REGULAR SCHOOLS

Local boards of education unable to adequately supply teachers to their alternative education programs can turn to staff repositioning as a solution. Moving regular school teachers during extended planning periods to alternative education classrooms is an effective practice in human resource development. Teachers serve as instructors in their subject areas for the portion of time alloted to repositioning before returning to their own classrooms. In this manner, alternative education programs get certified instructors for their classes while the school system gets relief from the financial burden of hiring full-time teachers in each academic area.

REPOSITIONED STAFF FROM SOCIAL SERVICE AGENCIES

Under this type of arrangement, as a partnership agreement between the local board of education and various social service agencies, repositioned caseworkers are placed with alternative education programs, with office space, supplies, and clerical assistance provided by the school system. Usually, caseworkers can be repositioned by changing their caseloads to include all students. This method allows caseworkers to more efficiently work with students in their natural environment while providing a service to alternative education. If done properly, repositioning requires no additional expenditures from the social service agency providing services. This practice appears to be a win-win situation for both the social service agency and the school system.

MATERIAL RESOURCE DEVELOPMENT

> Using grant funds, school sponsors, and school partners for material resource development instead of a total local commitment is an effective practice in alternative education.

Human resource development is only the beginning for school systems putting together alternative education programs. Material resource development demands immediate attention after staffing is complete. For example, staff members need office supplies, equipment, furniture, curricular materials, and instructional supplies. Material resource development (Figure 5.4) needs to address each of these areas before any funding proposal is drafted. In addition to staffing, discussed previously, many outside funding sources have categories for material resources.

In addition to local funds and grant funds, school sponsors and school partners can be used to assist with material resource development. Either of these sources is an excellent example of additional commitments or sources of matching funds often required by grant providers. Plus, local boards of education like sponsors and partners because they remove a large part of the financial burden from local taxpayers.

Locally Funded Resources

As stated before, securing local school system funding for alternative education programs is not easy. Alternative education programs that can boast of local funding are rare. Instead, local board of education members, fearing an additional taxpayer burden, often search for other means of funding material resources for their alternative education programs.

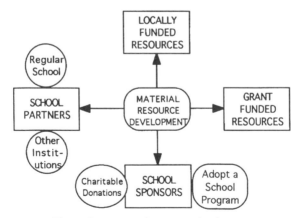

Figure 5.4 *Material resource development.*

Grant-Funded Resources

School systems often look to grants as sources of funding for material resources for their alternative education programs. Grants for this purpose are rewarded with few or no matching funds required by the local school system. Unlike human resources, material resources are usually considered for one-time funding, with no future obligation. Local school systems successful at landing grants for material resources enhance their programs without any financial risk. Grant funds are worthwhile for aspiring alternative education programs looking for ways to fund their material resource needs.

Use of School Sponsors

Use of school sponsors for the purpose of securing material resources is a "win-win" situation for all involved. The school system receiving charitable contributions from local agencies or engaged in adopt-a-school programs with local businesses win as a result of the "freebies" showered upon them. Sponsors win as a result of the positive publicity and public relations that result from their good deeds.

CHARITABLE DONATIONS

Contacting non-profit agencies, civic organizations, or private citizens for charitable donations to the alternative education program is an effective practice in material resource development. Sources providing cash contributions, purchasing materials for one-time gifts, or donating new or used material resources make no long-term commitment. There is no risk involved in approaching these individuals and groups for assistance. It is often their objective to lend a helping hand to those in need or for a good cause. The hardest part of this strategy may be finding the time to approach contributors. Certainly, it won't be hard to make a case for the need for contributions. Students at-risk and/or in alternative placement are of interest to everybody.

ADOPT-A-SCHOOL PROGRAMS

When local school systems are seeking long-term sponsorship for their alternative education programs, adopt-a-school programs should be considered. Local businesses, civic organizations, community agencies, and government offices make excellent adopt-a-school partners. Upon becoming an adopt-a-school partner, participants agree to offer long-term support, usually through a contractual agreement or written plan. Support in the form of material resources includes financing for equipment, furniture, office and instructional supplies, or direct donations of materials. Ideally, businesses specializing in products needed by the alternative education program should be sought as partners. For example, a local office supply business would make an ideal partner for the alternative education program, as would a local furniture or department store.

Use of School Partners

The use of regular public schools or other institutions as partners for alternative education programs is another effective practice in material resource development. Schools already fully operational have a multitude of resources that can be shared with or donated to the alternative education program. This practice requires no additional direct expense. Instead, it is an indirect method of providing material resources to alternative education programs. As an added bonus, this type of partnership provides an important link between regular and alternative education, a relationship that is lacking in many school systems around the country.

REGULAR SCHOOLS

Alternative education programs need not look far for assistance with material resource development. Tapping into the resources of regular public schools in close proximity to the alternative education facility has its advantages. Regular schools, acting as partners, can provide facilities missing from the alternative education site. For example, use of libraries, gymnasiums, auditoriums, and cafeterias can provide important services to students unable to obtain them otherwise. Most often, alternative education programs rely on regular schools for the use of audiovisual materials, surplus instructional materials, and used furniture. Separate alternative education programs usually rely on regular schools to prepare and transport meals for their students.

OTHER INSTITUTIONS

Private schools and institutions of higher learning have also been known to assist alternative education programs with material resource development. For example, in a type of partnership agreement, private schools and institutions of higher learning have agreed to provide furnishings and equipment to alternative education classrooms in exchange for use of the facilities during the evening or weekend hours. Institutions of higher learning are also excellent sources for providing alternative education programs with career education and vocational materials.

FROM PROGRAM PROPOSAL TO FUNDING PROPOSAL

> The program proposal can be transformed to a funding proposal with a minimum of changes and adjustments.

Unlike program proposals, which are submitted to the board of education for tentative program approval, funding proposals are used to apply for grants and financial sponsorships for the approved alternative program. The program proposal, however, can be transformed to a funding proposal with a minimum of changes and adjustments in content.

For the most part, a program proposal is a general outline detailing operational plans for alternative education programs. In review, program proposals should include an abstract of the program; the needs assessment data; the goals, objectives, and activities pertaining to the development, implementation, and evaluation domains; the facilities study; and the tentative budget.

A funding proposal, on the other hand, requires school systems to provide more in-depth and detailed information about program planning, development, implementation, and evaluation. Often, this task is undertaken by the collaborative team. As discussed previously, the collaborative team is a governing body consisting of a variety of local stakeholders, usually mandated as a stipulation for funding.

Most funding proposals require that this governing body also oversee the day-to-day operations of the alternative education program once

grants have been awarded and the funding cycle has begun. This requirement is most easily achieved by transplanting members of the existing
planning committee to a collaborative team. Power can be transferred to
members of the new governing body after desired changes in membership are made. Changes may occur through the addition of new members
or deletion of planning committee positions not conducive to the mission
of the collaborative team.

> The initial program proposal may be compared to a plan-
> ning blueprint showing the general structure and frame-
> work of a house to be built. Upon approval of this proposal,
> a more specific, detailed plan is initiated by its stakeholders
> to furnish, operate, and finance the household once devel-
> opment is complete.

Once a funding proposal has been developed by the collaborative team,
the funding institution will evaluate it for completion and acccuracy.
Hefner-Packer (1991, p. 37) listed the following criteria used to evaluate
alternative education program proposals:

- mission of proposed alternative program
- compatibility with funding source guidelines
- effect on current policies and procedures
- available resources (human, material, financial)
- resources required for implementation
- cost effectiveness
- advantages/disadvantages

REFERENCE

Hefner-Packer, R. 1991. "Alternative education programs: A prescription for success,"
    Monographs in Education, Vol. 12, C. T. Holmes (Ed.). Athens, GA: College of
    Education, University of Georgia.

Chapter 6

THE IMPLEMENTATION DOMAIN: CURRICULAR PRACTICES

> Give a man a fish and you feed him for a day. Teach a man to fish and you feed him for a lifetime.

Curricular practices in alternative education often involve diverse and innovative resources not typically used in regular school settings. The alternative curriculum is more effective with students at-risk when comprehensive in nature, encompassing all aspects of students' current and future functioning and skill attainment. The comprehensive curriculum shown in Figure 6.1 includes affective education, career education, life skills education, and leisure education in addition to the basic skills and academic enrichment.

Not unlike the essentialism movement in education, the curriculum must make the basic skills required for high school completion a high priority. In addition, academic enrichment, life skills, career education, affective education, and leisure education expands the traditional basic skills of reading, writing, and arithmetic into a sort of "new basic skills" curriculum.

Philosophically speaking, innovative curricular practices in alternative education are typically patterned after the progressivism movement in education. Ryan and Cooper (1995) found that "progressive teachers often use traditional subject matter, but use it differently from the way it is used in a traditional classroom. Progressives believe that the value of knowledge is found in its ability to solve human problems" (p. 130).

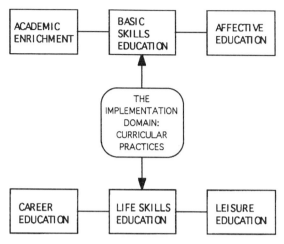

Figure 6.1 *Curricular practices.*

Alternative educators believe that students can learn problem-solving skills from a conflict-resolution course just as well as from a mathematics course. Therefore, alternative educators strive to emphasize both the academic basic skills and the "new basic skills" necessary for comprehensive, well-rounded growth and development.

BASIC SKILLS EDUCATION

Basic skills instruction has been found to be effective when the curriculum is sequential, when objectives are competency-based, when instruction is delivered with the aid of related multimedia, and when all subjects are covered through an emphasis on reading, writing, and arithmetic.

Conceptual Background

Slavin, Karweit, and Madden (1989) contended that we must organize schools differently if we are to be successful in helping students attain an adequate level of basic skills. They suggested that a plan be in place at all grade levels to ensure that students achieve success at each step in their schooling. Such a plan could include provisions for alternative education programs due to their reputation for offering a different delivery system. Preventive and remedial programs included in these plans are effective if they are intensive, assess student progress, adapt instruction to individual needs, and are comprehensive in nature.

Hamby (1989) advocated the development of continuous-progress mastery approaches to instruction in basic skills to avoid grade retention of students. These approaches include individualized, self-paced, competency-based instruction with monitoring and feedback. McLaughlin and Vacha (1992) found that teachers can sequence skill introduction, present new competency-based concepts directly, provide modeling and examples from a variety of multimedia materials, guide repeated practice, and test for mastery in all the subjects including writing, reading, and arithmetic (Figure 6.2).

The Concept in Practice

In the lab school setting, basic skills are approached in a sequential manner, from the simple to the more complex. Organized through competency objectives, skills are broken down into small, manageable

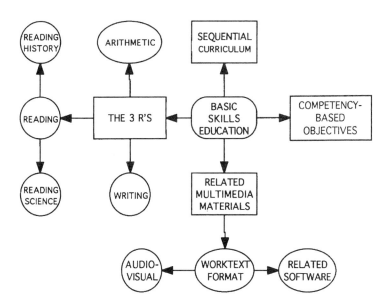

Figure 6.2 Basic skills education.

bits. Each skill is taught using related multimedia instructional materials, such as worktexts instead of traditional textbooks, related software, and audiovisual support. Related multimedia materials have been found by this author to enhance learning opportunities for the visual, hands-on learner.

THE THREE R's

Traditionally, reading, writing, and arithmetic have been the mainstay of the basic skills movement in education. Throw in science and social studies for good measure and you have an essentialist's dream. Making these subjects interesting and relevant is the real challenge—just the kind of challenge this alternative educator was looking for when founding the Institute for Effective Practices in Alternative Education. Here is what was found to be effective in the lab school setting.

READING

In an effort to devote enough time to the development of reading skills, students were scheduled for reading instruction through their regular English classes and for practice through content area reading in their science and social studies classes. Content area science and social studies involved reading and analyzing stories about various topics in the two disciplines. Meanwhile, students also received credit for learning reading in their English classes. This adaptation allows students who are poor readers to practice reading several times a day without sacrificing a major subject. Content area reading is surprisingly economical from the standpoint of time and investment of resources. It is also a low-profile method of improving reading skills.

WRITING

Emphasizing writing more than reading has been found to be effective in the lab school setting due to Glasser's (1992) theory that "anyone who can write well can read well, but many who can read well can hardly write" (p. 229). The Institute of Effective Practices in Alternative Education suggests that one start young when asking students to write words, sentences, and paragraphs, leading up to more extensive writing assignments, such as a daily journal. This author used the journal method with alternative education students in the lab school setting as a means of getting students to write. For example, journal writing was used as a "sponge" activity at strategic times during the school day, such as before school, after lunch, when waiting for class to begin, or after school.

ARITHMETIC

Since mathematics is a continuous course progressing from one level to the next, students in the lab school setting start with basic arithmetic and are asked to show the mathematics teacher the level at which they are competent. The level at which a particular student shows competence is that student's starting point. Students progress at their own rate and move ahead as they show competence. Students are allowed to ask peers or staff members for help at any time.

LEISURE EDUCATION

> Providing students with a newspaper-in-education program, opportunities for journal writing, personal development experiences, and enrichment retreats are effective practices in leisure education.

Conceptual Background

Recreation and leisure are important activities in American society. Gibson and Mitchell (1986) stated, "We need but pause to consider the amount of time, money, and effort we expend in these pursuits to recognize their significance in our lives. . . . The interrelationships between a 'career' and a 'way of life' cannot ignore the role of recreation and leisure in the latter" (p. 355).

Alternative educators concerned with the total well-being of their students must become more sensitive to the role and potential of leisure time activities for enhancing their students' quality of life now and in the future. It is well documented that leisure time activities have great transfer effect on activities in later life. Leisure activities offer a mix of challenges, relaxation, play, entertainment, socialization, and constructiveness leading to a more balanced life. In the case of students, leisure activities complement or compensate for other life involvements, such as work, family, and the peer group (Gibson & Mitchell, 1986).

The Concept in Practice

A multitude of leisure activities are available today. When teaching students leisure activities, alternative educators must choose those that are accessible for their particular situation. The Institute of Effective Practices in Alternative Education has found the newspaper, personal journal writing, healthy lifestyles class, physical development, and student enrichment retreats leisure activities that are effective with alternative education students (Figure 6.3).

NEWSPAPER IN EDUCATION

The newspaper is an excellent tool for motivating students to learn in the lab school setting. Even the most resistant readers turn eagerly to the sports pages, the entertainment listings, the teen section, or the front page account of a catastrophic event. As an alternative to traditional textbooks, the newspaper acts as a reading incentive and a source of practical information about life, not to mention its transfer potential as a lifelong

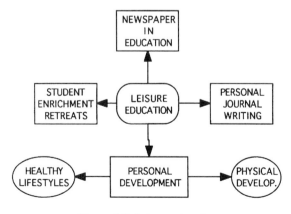

Figure 6.3 *Leisure education.*

leisure activity. The Institute of Effective Practices in Alternative Education considers the newspaper the most underrated tool and best kept secret in education.

PERSONAL JOURNAL WRITING

In the lab school setting, this author has deescalated the emphasis on reading while escalating the emphasis on writing, consistent with Glasser's philosophy that anyone who can write well can read well. Students are asked to practice writing words, then sentences, paragraphs, and finally journal passages as a means improving both reading and writing. Students in the lab school setting are asked to keep a personal journal, making an entry on a daily basis. Students are free to write on any topic, similar to the personal diaries that many people keep. Due to their similarity to personal diaries, personal journals have direct transfer potential to lifelong learning.

PERSONAL DEVELOPMENT

In most states, physical education and health are required courses, at least through the ninth grade. Due to a lack of facilities, adaptive physical education and health programs are commonplace for many alternative education programs. Personal development in alternative education involves experiences in both physical development and healthy life styles.

Healthy Lifestyles

As an alternative to general health classes in the traditional sense, health in the lab school setting involves lifestyle issues affecting alternative education students. Health topics found effective with alternative education students, particularly those served for a short period of time, include self-esteem, substance abuse, stress, sexuality, emotional management, interpersonal relationships, etc. It is this author's belief that critical issues pertaining to students' identified problem areas need to be addressed if we are to elicit improvement while students are enrolled in alternative education programs.

Physical Development

While physical development is an important lifelong leisure activity, it is also an important part of a physical education program. The majority of alternative education programs are based in retired elementary schools or community buildings and, therefore, lack physical education facilities. The lab school setting is no exception. With no on-site facilities for physical education, creative alternatives are necessary. In the lab school, a large unoccupied classroom has been transformed into a resistance training facility. Students helped develop the facility as a school project, and now participate in a structured training program on a daily basis. Through donations and salvage restoration of equipment, the program very successfully provides students with an adapted method of physical development.

STUDENT ENRICHMENT RETREATS

Providing students with off-campus enrichment retreats is an effective method of facilitating responsibility, leadership, and self-esteem. Students from the lab school participated in overnight camping retreats designed to tap leadership potential through a variety of workshops and group activities. Some students had never been away from the local community before participating in the retreats. The outdoor-oriented retreats effectively transfer to lifelong leisure and recreational activities, such as camping, fishing, and hiking.

LIFE SKILLS EDUCATION

Teaching students to communicate effectively through opportunities for public speaking, to prevent and resolve conflicts responsibly, to learn about the law and juvenile justice, and to solve problems by making positive decisions are effective practices in life skills education.

Conceptual Background

Edgar (1989) recommended using mini-courses to teach life skills to students. Such courses can be designed as supplementary activities to which students are not exposed during academic classes. Edgar suggested that mini-courses be presented by monitors, teachers, or resource personnel.

In the lab school setting, mini-courses were offered in the areas of public speaking, juvenile justice and the law, preventing and resolving conflicts, and making positive choices through the decision-making and problem-solving processes (Figure 6.4). Depending on the results of individual needs assessments and program evaluations, additional mini-courses may be developed that are appropriate for a school system's particular situation. Of the life skills listed above, Glasser (1992) found speaking the most important, even though it is an almost totally neglected part of the curriculum in almost all schools. Glasser stated:

> Even from our best schools, the vast majority of students who graduate have almost no ability to speak competently on an intellectual subject. Since success in almost every field, as well as in our personal lives, depends on the ability to speak clearly and sensibly, every teacher in the quality school would focus on teaching students this skill and giving them a lot of opportunity to practice it. All students who graduated from a Quality School would be able to speak well. (pp. 288–289)

The Concept in Practice

Life skills mini-courses can be offered in a variety of areas. Based on needs assessment results, the lab school staff selected public speaking, juvenile justice and the law, preventing and resolving conflicts, and

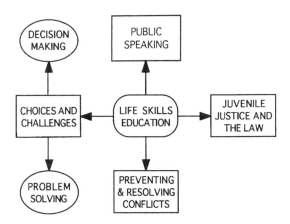

Figure 6.4 Life skills education.

problem-solving and decision-making skills as mini-courses for its alternative education students.

PUBLIC SPEAKING

In the spirit of Glasser's belief that speaking is the most important part of the curriculum, this author provides lab school students with experience in public speaking throughout the school year. Low-profile presentations and high-profile speeches are opportunities offered to students in a variety of formats. After the initial jitters, students usually become acclimated to speaking effectively in front of others, facilitating improvement along the way.

JUVENILE JUSTICE AND THE LAW

As a result of needs assessment and the large population of adjudicated youth in the lab school setting, training in juvenile justice and the law is provided. Providing students not presently adjudicated with the same coursework allows the program to take a proactive approach to preventing juvenile crime. Students are exposed to both criminal justice and civil justice while assigned to this class. Successful completion of the course is a requirement for all students in the lab school setting, since becoming knowledgeable about our legal system is considered a critical life skill for all individuals.

PREVENTING AND RESOLVING CONFLICTS

Conflict prevention and resolution are also considered critical life skill areas for youth. Both are utilized in the lab school setting as requirements in place of a regular school elective. Students are trained as peer mediators, and learn negotiating skills along the way. Anger management becomes a focal point when discussing ways to diffuse conflict. A conflict resolution room is in the works at the lab school site. Identified conflicts can be mediated or negotiated in this center as a means of providing a quiet, private place to conduct counseling and conflict resolution skills.

CHOICES AND CHALLENGES: DECISION MAKING AND PROBLEM SOLVING

Teaching decision-making and problem-solving skills in the lab school setting has been an effective practice with alternative education students. Both skills are critical to successful living, and are used constantly throughout life. Students learn these skills through exploration and role playing, practicing what they have learned using specific scenarios and situations. Students are presented with step-by-step problem-solving and decision-making models for use in role plays and modeling activities.

AFFECTIVE EDUCATION

> Addressing citizenship and civics, character of the individual, clarification of values, and personal and social adjustment are effective practices in affective education.

Conceptual Background

According to Dinkmeyer, Pew, and Dinkmeyer (1979), in many classrooms the affective domain is ignored in the rush to "return to the basics." Developing an understanding of self and others should be a central goal in alternative education programs. It is universally accepted that academic achievement is highly correlated with positive feelings and self-worth. Dinkmeyer et al. contended that our curriculum must include an affective component to assist the child in developing this understanding of self and others. Understanding of self and others can be accomplished through the development of citizenship and civic pride, an emphasis on character education, values clarification, and the facilitation of personal and social adjustment in students (Figure 6.5).

The Concept in Practice

Affective education in the lab school setting takes place during an afternoon block of periods after a morning block of academics. The topics shown in Figure 6.5 cover a broad area of affective education. By no means are these areas inclusive or written in stone. Other programs may take different directions or modify the topics discussed below to more effectively fit their needs.

CITIZENSHIP AND CIVIC PRIDE

As part of the affective education program in the lab school setting, students are exposed to citizenship and civics education and are then asked to participate in a school/community project as a means of applying what they learned in the classroom. Projects range from volunteer work to neighborhood cleanup initiatives. Finally, students are asked to analyze and describe their experiences while participating in the project.

CHARACTER EDUCATION

In an effort to pass on to our students the best of our culture's values, the lab school staff vigorously teaches the positive moral values embedded in our society. Instead of having students simply study the facts or read a story, the teachers confront them with ethical dilemmas and moral lessons that are integral to the subject matter. Students role play or model specific dilemmas and situations in order to facilitate learning and transfer of learning.

VALUES CLARIFICATION

In practice, values clarification seeks to assist the individual in developing better self-understanding and a positive self-concept, in making appropriate decisions and meaningful choices, and in satisfactorily adjusting to the demands of everyday living. A counselor coordinates group values exercises designed to facilitate self-assessment, self-concept

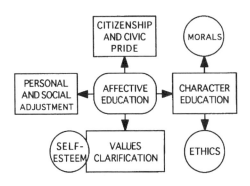

Figure 6.5 *Affective education.*

clarification, and reinforcement of change. Also, exercises give students the opportunity to compare, examine, and defend their behavior, values, and interests against the norms of others.

PERSONAL AND SOCIAL ADJUSTMENT

In practice, courses in personal and social adjustment require students to complete prescribed learning packets addressing all the identified problem areas experienced at home, school, and in the peer group. Students are required to complete a self-assessment and analysis of their particular situation. Self-analysis should result in an adjustment plan developed by the student with the support of staff members. The plan is put into action as part of the student's ongoing adjustment initiative. Plans that are modified periodically are particularly effective in facilitating adjustment in students over time.

CAREER EDUCATION

> Preparing students for the world of work through career exploration and planning, and providing them with opportunities for work study or an internship experience in a vocation of interest are effective practices in career education.

Emphasizing workplace readiness and career exploration and planning helps students prepare for a productive future in the world of work. Entering students in paid work study or vocational internships gives them the practical experience and exposure necessary to make future employment and career decisions (Figure 6.6).

Career Exploration and Planning

CONCEPTUAL BACKGROUND

Isaacson (1985) emphasized the use of interest inventory results as the major means of determining occupational options, describing several interest inventories that are keyed directly to occupational options. Clients are often inclined to focus attention on interest scores to confirm their subjective evaluations and then move their attention to occupations named by those scores. Interest inventories and the resulting occupational options can help at-risk students identify career goals early in high school, thereby increasing their chances of completing high school.

Beck (1991) found that school personnel, especially guidance counselors, can be a significant factor in keeping students in school by assisting them in making career choices. Beck suggests that counselors can also coordinate orientation for preemployment awareness, training in life, coping and work readiness skills, and entry into the job market. Successful career programs are characterized by cooperation with business leaders, intensive student counseling, practical work experience, and training in basic skills needed for success on a job.

THE CONCEPT IN PRACTICE

In practice, career exploration and planning occurs in advance of placement in a work study program or vocational internship. Career exploration and planning is a prerequisite to workplace readiness. Exploring career fields, interests, and qualifications are initial practices in the career exploration and planning process. Next in the process is the administration of interest and personality inventories to all students. Characteristics identified through the inventories are then

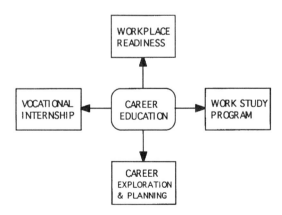

Figure 6.6 *Career education.*

matched to careers in an effort to provide students with the means to beginplanning.

Workplace Readiness

CONCEPTUAL BACKGROUND

Are students leaving school ready to go to work? Mark Newton, Director of Organizational Development for Cincinnati Gas and Electric, stated, "A workforce that possesses both technical competence and employability skills is no luxury—it's a necessity." In today's changing workplace, technical skills are a must. But career success depends on workers being able to adapt quickly and effectively to new demands and expectations.

What Work Requires of Schools, a SCANS Report for Americal 2000, identified problem solving, teamwork, and self-management as essential competencies, skills, and personal qualities for all students—both those going directly to work and those planning further education. Paul O'Neill, Chairman of the President's Education Policy Advisory Committee, stated, "This report goes well beyond 'the basics.' It provides a fresh and, above all, realistic look at the new and different kinds of skills and knowledge workers need in today's workplace—and need to be able to adapt to tomorrow's workplace" (Agency for Instructional Technology, 1994, p. 5).

WORKPLACE READINESS IN PRACTICE

In practice, workplace readiness in alternative education is facilitated through teaching employability skills to students. In the lab school setting, students have been taught problem-solving, teamwork, and self-sufficiency skills to enhance their employability in the future. These skills are taught in other areas of the lab school program as well. This is not unusual for progressive alternative education programs, however, as they are typically on the "cutting edge" when it comes to providing students with usable skills.

Workplace readiness follows career exploration and planning as a means of preparing students for employablility in their field of choice. At this point, students in the lab school setting are provided opportunities for employment so that they can gain practical work experience before leaving school.

Work Study Program

CONCEPTUAL BACKGROUND

Mackey and Appleman (1983) maintained that adolescents are likely to be more attached to their jobs than to school. They contend, therefore, that as work becomes more pervasive in adolescent society, it should be incorporated into the school curriculum. In language arts, for example, students can write resumes and letters of application. Similarly, social studies classes should analyze job trends and the sociology of work. Work experiences for students can also become part of the total school program in the form of paid work study programs or volunteer internships.

WORK STUDY IN PRACTICE

In practice, students of proper age are placed in paid employment positions as part of a work study program. Students in the lab school are provided with career exploration and planning, and workplace readiness training during part of the regular school day. After completing required courses, students either report to work or return home before reporting to work in the evening. Students keep time logs, experience journals, and evaluation forms during their work study experience. Staffers visit the job site once weekly for evaluation purposes.

Vocational Internship

CONCEPTUAL BACKGROUND

Walls (1990) advocated a cooperative partnership between schools and local businesses in an effort to provide work experiences for youth. Young potential employees are supplied to businesses in return for giving individual attention and future opportunities for entry level employment to students who might otherwise have dropped out of school. Students are assigned a mentor from the participating business along with an internship in the company. The business gives the students on-the-job training and assists with career exploration. In return, the school system agrees to train the businesses' employees in mentoring skills and help them know what to expect from the students in the program.

VOCATIONAL INTERNSHIP IN PRACTICE

In practice, students too young for regular paid employment are provided with an internship experience in an effort to provide them with work experience. In the lab school setting, students are rotated through several internship experiences over the course of the year. Every six weeks, students move to a different type of work by acting as trainees in fields such as nursing, child care, retail sales, secretarial, clerical, teaching, and legal services. By year's end, each student has been exposed to several different career fields, while benefitting from the mentoring, leadership, and responsibility they have experienced.

ACADEMIC ENRICHMENT

> Giving students the opportunity to complete major projects, deliver presentations, participate in exploratory activities, and use audiovisuals are effective practices in academic enrichment.

Conceptual Background

Boyer (1987) utilized student recognition programs, after-school workshops, and summer enrichment sessions designed to meet the needs of children and their families. He contends that new enrichment programs, which are part of the extended school day, should be an option for all students. Boyer emphasizes that the enrichment programs would provide the option for children from all social and economic backgrounds to participate together.

Figure 6.7 illustrates the type of enrichment activities that are available to students before, during, and after school, as well as in a summer program. Enrichment activities recognize and extend students' abilities while facilitating learning in the different academic disciplines.

The Concept in Practice

In practice, academic enrichment entails the incorporation of supplemental activities designed to enhance the learning process through creative means. Enrichment activities found effective with alternative education students include audiovisual-based learning, major projects, classroom presentations, and exploratory/discovery opportunities. Depending on individual circumstances, other enrichment activities may be useful for a particular program.

COMPLETING MAJOR PROJECTS

Giving alternative education students an opportunity to complete major projects in the different academic disciplines is an effective practice in academic enrichment. Students in the lab school setting are presented with topics to research and display in project form and are provided with project boards and materials to use for the display. Topics range from a particular research problem to a famous historical figure. When completed, major projects are displayed in the hallways after students have presented them to the class.

DELIVERING PRESENTATIONS

Students in the lab school setting are provided periodic opportunities to deliver presentations to the class. Presentation formats include

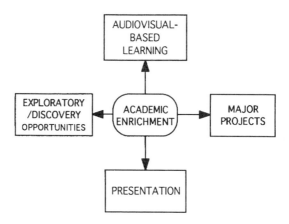

Figure 6.7 *Academic enrichment.*

speeches and demonstration. Topics are variable, and range from reports on important figures to research findings. Presentations are videotaped as a method of providing feedback to students about their performance. Students are taught the characteristics of effective presenting and encouraged to deliver presentations both individually and as a team with other students.

PARTICIPATING IN EXPLORATORY ACTIVITIES

Students in the lab school setting are presented with exploratory opportunities in the different academic disciplines. Creative problem solving and experiential learning are encouraged through various exploratory projects in science, social studies, math, and English. Science labs, math problems, social studies topics, and reading and writing explorations are easily initiated using problem-solving, decision-making, and critical thinking skills.

USING AUDIOVISUALS

Audiovisuals are used in the lab school setting to supplement the use of print material and computer-assisted instruction. Audiovisuals provide a visual picture of learning topics, as well as a different mode of learning to reinforce concepts and details. Audiovisuals effectively present material not easily assimilated by students from print material.

REFERENCES

Agency for Instructional Technology. 1994. *Workplace Readiness: Education for Employment.* Bloomington, IN: AIT.

Beck, M. S. 1991. "Increasing school completion: Strategies that work," *Monographs in Education, Vol. 13,* C. T. Holmes (Ed.). Athens, GA: College of Education, University of Georgia.

Boyer, E. L. 1987. "Early schooling and the nation's future," *Educational Leadership,* 44(6):4–6.

Dinkmeyer, D. C., Pew, W. L., & Dinkmeyer, D. C., Jr. 1979. *Adlerian Counseling and Psychotherapy.* Monterey, CA: Brooks/Cole, p. 311.

Edgar, S. 1989. "An analysis of the effects of an intervention program on academic, social, and personal adjustment of at-risk and retained seventh and eighth grade students" (Doctoral dissertation, Northern Arizona University, 1987), *Dissertation Abstracts International,* 49:7920A.

Georgia Department of Education. 1995. *Workplace Readiness: Education for Employment.* Bloomington, IN: Agency for Instructional Technology.

Gibson, R. L., & Mitchell, M. H. 1986. *Introduction to Counseling and Guidance.* New York: Macmillan Publishing Company.

Glasser, W., M.D. 1992. *The Quality School: Managing Students without Coercion.* New York: Harper Perennial Publishers, pp. 226–236.

Hamby, J. V. 1989. "How to get an "A" on your dropout prevention report card," *Educational Leadership,* 46(5):21–28.

Isaacson, L. E. 1985. *Basics of Career Counseling.* Boston, MA: Allyn & Bacon, Inc.

Mackey, J., & Appleman, D. 1983. "The growth of adolescent apathy," *Educational Leadership,* 40(6):30–33.

McLaughlin, T. F., & Vacha, E. F. 1992. "School programs for at-risk children and youth: A review," *Education and Treatment of Children,* 15(3):255–267.

Ryan, K., & J. M. Cooper. 1995. *Those Who Can Teach.* Boston, MA: Houghton Mifflin Co., pp. 130–137.

Slavin, R. E., Karweit, N. L., & Madden, N. A. 1989. *Effective Programs for Students at Risk.* Needham Heights, MA: Allyn & Bacon.

Walls, M. W. 1990. "The promise of a job keeps dropout-prone kids in school," *The Executive Educator,* 12(4):22–23.

Chapter 7

THE IMPLEMENTATION DOMAIN: INSTRUCTIONAL PRACTICES

> You cannot teach a man anything; you can only help him find it within himself.
>
> —*Galileo*

Instructional practices in alternative education often include diverse and innovative strategies in the areas of student placement, classroom management, teaching and learning, and student evaluation (Figure 7.1). Due to differences in the learning style and personal background of individual students, diversity in instructional practices is a necessary component of alternative education programs.

Philosophically speaking, instructional practices in alternative education are typically patterned after the progressivism movement in education. "Progressive educators believe that the place to begin an education is with the student, rather than with the subject matter. . . . Rather than being a presenter of knowledge or a taskmaster, the teacher is an intellectual guide, a facilitator in the problem-solving process. Students are encouraged to be imaginative and resourceful in solving problems" (Ryan & Cooper, 1995, p. 130).

Existentialism has also impacted alternative education. Existentialism is grounded historically in the human potential movement and moral education. Existentialism is "a point of view that influences all that the teacher teaches and how he or she teaches. It tries to engage the child in central questions of defining life. It attempts to help the child acknowledge his or her own freedom and accept the responsibility for that freedom" (Ryan & Cooper, 1995, p. 137).

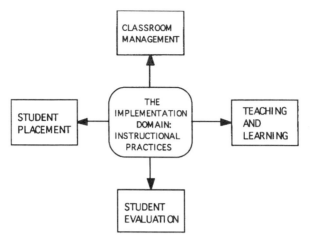

Figure 7.1 Instructional practices.

STUDENT PLACEMENT

As a throwback to the days of the one-room schoolhouse approach to grouping, students in grades 6–12 are provided with assessment and an individualized education plan before placement in subject specific learning centers. Cross-grade grouping is an effective practice in student placement for programs with a small number of teachers teaching students in both middle and high school grades.

Conceptual Background

Student placement is the first step in the instructional practices domain in alternative education. Student placement is extremely challenging due to the number of grades and schools served, types of students, and availability of teachers in most alternative education programs. The majority of programs take on the look of a one-room schoolhouse due to the presence of both middle- and high-school students in the program. Learning centers must provide both cognitive and affective educational experiences to students placed through cross-grade grouping strategies (Figure 7.2).

The Concept in Practice

In practice, the one-room schoolhouse approach is used to house either self-contained or rotating groups of students, depending on the number of teachers available. In the lab school setting, both formats have been tried as the number of teachers has increased.

First, students were self-contained in learning centers of up to fifteen students each. Here, all cognitive and affective courses were taught, with a multicertified teacher assigned to provide the bulk of instruction. Students were not afforded the luxury of class change, and teachers were forced to teach several different subjects during the day, not unlike the historic one-room schoolhouse. Later, due to the addition of teachers, students were able to experience class change as four learning centers each housed a different major subject. Having individual English, math, science, and social studies learning centers made it possible for the lab school to become more specialized.

Out of necessity, each of four homeroom groups of students moved together from one learning center to the next. By noon, students had spent a period in each major subject. After lunch, students were self-contained by grade level for affective education instruction. This format allowed staffers to use both the self-contained and rotating schedules at various times during the day. Both formats have been found effective for totally different reasons. Self-containment fosters a more nurturing, controlled

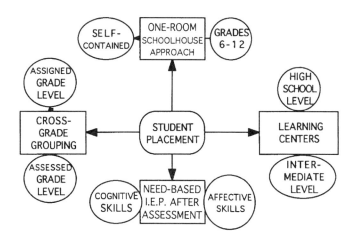

Figure 7.2 *Student placement.*

environment, while class change breeds self-responsibility and adaptability to different situations. Several lab school components serve as transitional programs to regular schools. Thus, the "class change" format provides transitional skills for students in these programs.

On the other hand, school choice programs in the lab school setting utilize the self-contained format more extensively due to the presence of a nurturing, structured environment. Opportunities for open class change, self-governance, flexible scheduling, and a variety of privileges are effective with students attending alternative programs by choice. Students who are able to choose typically require less structure than students in alternative placement by assignment.

Providing students enrolled in alternative programs of choice the opportunity for open class changes, self-governance, flexible scheduling, and a variety of privileges are effective practices in alternative education.

CLASSROOM MANAGEMENT

Providing students with consistency through classroom dynamics, a "level system" of classroom management, opportunities for behavioral engineering, and peer mentors are all effective practices in alternative education.

Consistency is the most critical ingredient in effective classroom management. Effective classroom dynamics with respect to teacher and group behavior is facilitated by consistency in classroom management. Consistency can be enhanced through a sequential four-step process referred to as the "level system." Students participate in behavioral engineering in advance of placement in the level system, and thereafter when warranted by misbehavior. In addition, peer mentors are assigned to students in an effort to enhance consistency and positive student behavior. Figure 7.3 breaks down these innovative classroom management techniques suggested for alternative education programs.

Classroom Dynamics

CONCEPTUAL BACKGROUND

Dinkmeyer, Pew, and Dinkmeyer (1979) suggested that every classroom has its own unique classroom dynamics, recommending that the teacher take advantage of positive group forces in the classroom. During the course of classroom management, the teacher may become aware of interrelationships among children. In addition, teachers should foster interrelationships among themselves and their students. Dinkmeyer et al. offered the classroom meeting as an example of a technique that recognizes the value of the classroom as a group and provides a democratic format for problem solving.

THE CONCEPT IN PRACTICE

In practice, incorporating democratic principles as part of a classroom management plan is an effective way of utilizing group dynamics. Interrelationships among students and their teachers in the lab school

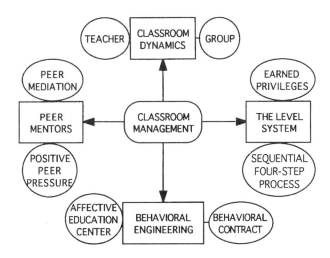

Figure 7.3 *Classroom management.*

setting are an important part of their classroom management strategy. Students and teachers communicate, interact, make decisions, and problem-solve together regularly. This practice has resulted in improved student performance and self-esteem.

The Level System of Classroom Management

Classroom management entails using behavioral procedures for the prevention of and intervention in misbehavior. The level system of classroom management is an effective classroom prevention/intervention strategy that utilizes a sequential progression of promotional stages with built-in privileges at each level. Attainment of the highest level usually results in achievement of predetermined goals, such as grade promotion or return to the regular school environment.

CONCEPTUAL BACKGROUND

McLaughlin and Vacha (1992) found that behavioral procedures were effective as classroom intervention strategies with at-risk youth. They concluded that behavior analysis can help at-risk students with the necessary survival skills for school success. Teachers and paraprofessionals can be prepared to collect data in an ongoing manner to determine student/child progress. They can also be taught the basic principles of learning, trained to institute effective and systematic procedures, and required to state goals precisely (p. 261).

Wehlage, Rutter, and Turnbaugh (1987) advocated a program requiring a commitment from individual students. Students commit themselves to a set of rules, work expectations, and standards of behavior. Rules about attendance, the quantity and quality of work required, and the consequences for breaking rules need to be spelled out in detail. Wehlage et al. (1987) emphasized clear rules that all students need to observe if they are to keep their commitment. They contended that students should observe important ethical rules such as not stealing from others and not committing acts of violence (p. 72).

THE CONCEPT IN PRACTICE

In practice, students tracked through a "level system" of classroom management commit themselves to a set of rules, work expectations, and standards of behavior. The level system is effective both for students enrolled in the lab school by assignment and by choice.

Students enrolled by assignment who follow the rules and regulations, meet work expectations, and hold high standards of behavior are promoted through three additional levels before returning to the regular school environment. Beginning at the "entry level," students are given a fresh start toward getting an education. The entry level is simply a starting point at which a student is at "ground zero" in the point system. Having no points in this system is a good thing because termination points are given when a student breaks a rule or regulation at any level.

Upon being placed in a homeroom after meeting enrollment requirements, students are moved to level two, the adjustment level, where they stay as long as needed to make the kind of changes that lead to a return to the regular school. The goal is to keep oneself at ground zero in points.

Students who consistently remain at ground zero are promoted to level three, the model level. Students earning termination points due to violations of the rules and regulations remain at the adjustment level or are referred to a disciplinary panel or juvenile court. Model level students are required to demonstrate mature behavior and are given privileges that model the regular school environment. Earning too many T-points (termination points) at the model level results in demotion to the adjustment level for readjustment or referral to the disciplinary tribunal or juvenile court.

Students who consistently remain at ground zero while at the model level are promoted to the fourth and final level, the return level, which signals a return to regular school in the near future. Should a return level student earn too many T-points for violation of the rules and regulations, he or she is returned to the adjustment level to work back through the system a second time.

Students enrolled by choice in the lab school are also exposed to the level system of classroom management. Choice students are started at the model level upon enrollment and only experience the adjustment level if warranted by poor behavior, unsatisfactory work ethic, or both. Choice students may stay at the model level throughout their stay in the alternative education program since enrollment is usually long-term and voluntary.

Behavioral Engineering

Each person, even young children, can be viewed as having the creative capacity to decide and choose—all human behavior has a purpose. Therefore, purposiveness is probably the most important explanation of one's behavior and misbehavior. Only if alternative educators understand a child's mistaken behavior are they able to cooperatively plan with the child helpful approaches to purposeful behavior. If a teacher does not understand the logic behind a student's choice of goals, behavioral interventions may not produce significant change in behavior (Dinkmeyer, Pew, & Dinkmeyer, 1979).

The skills of encouragement and consistency, and the use of natural and logical consequences (instead of rewards and punishments), can assist alternative educators in their most important work—to engineer their students' behavioral development. As shown in Figure 7.3, behavioral contracting and use of an effective education center as a means of providing resources for use in "behavioral engineering" are effective practices in classroom management. Given the capacity for goal-directed, purposeful behavior, students develop the means to meet the social, interpersonal, and academic demands of the classroom, as well as those at home, work, or in the peer group.

Behavioral Contracting

Behavioral contracting is a classroom management technique used to structure the classroom rules and regulations, as well as to hold each student responsible for abiding by the contents of the contract. Each student is held accountable for his or her own actions when in violation of such a contract.

CONCEPTUAL BACKGROUND

According to Short (1988), behavioral contracting forces the student to take an active role in the classroom to which he/she is assigned. Negotiation of the contract may occur prior to entering the classroom or upon entry. Specifics of the contract depend on the reasons for referral. Persons drawing the contract with the student should have the appropriate knowledge and skills to do so. Students should be taught the importance of honoring a contract and for being responsible for carrying out its terms (p. 29).

THE CONCEPT IN PRACTICE

This author put the concept of behavioral contracting into practice by first having teachers assist individual students in developing a purposeful, goal-directed plan before entering the classroom. This plan resulted from an in-depth study and understanding of the particular student's prior behavior and background.

After cooperatively planning with the student approaches to purposeful, goal-directed behavior, behavioral contracting was used to structure the plan, and all students were required to sign a contract containing the rules, regulations, and procedures of the classroom. In the event the contract was not honored by the student, provisions were included for natural and logical consequences as these have been found to be more effective with students than rewards and punishments.

Affective Education Center

An affective education center is used to provide resources to teachers and space for them to send students for behavioral engineering sessions. When contracting and classroom efforts fall short of facilitating change in behavior, teachers can refer students to the center for counseling or behavioral planning.

CONCEPTUAL BACKGROUND

Dinkmeyer et al. (1979) reported that in many classrooms the affective domain is ignored in the rush to "return to the basics." Developing an understanding of self and others should be a central goal in the educational process. Dinkmeyer et al. contend that it is universally accepted that academic achievement is highly correlated with positive feelings and self-worth. As a result, our schools must include an affective component to assist the child in developing an understanding of self and others.

THE CONCEPT IN PRACTICE

This author decided to implement an affective center in the lab school setting as an innovative method of putting affective education into practice. The center was used as a hub for affective education resources, planning, and counseling services. Behavioral intervention was carried out in the center by either an administrator, counselor, or teacher. The term "behavioral engineering" surfaced as a result of the structured methods used to plan for purposeful, goal-directed behavior on the part of students. Behavioral engineering is an ongoing process of planning, implementing, and revising behavior strategies for misbehaving students.

Peer Mentors

The practice of peer mentoring in alternative education classrooms should begin to increase in popularity as the number of multilevel programs increase around the nation. Alternative educators can use peer mentoring to enhance their classroom management programs while empowering students to help each other.

CONCEPTUAL BACKGROUND

Bronfenbrenner (1986) described a mentor as someone with a skill that he or she wishes to teach to a younger person. "We don't make much use of mentors in U.S. society, and we don't give much recognition or encouragement to individuals who play this important role. As a result, many U.S. children have few significant and committed adults in their lives" (Bronfenbrenner, 1986, p. 430). Branfenbrenner concluded that, most often, their mentors are a significant other or older classmate.

Peer mentoring has been described as a systematic accounting system for monitoring and assisting students. For example, Hamby (1989) discussed the development of a systematic accounting system for monitoring of student absences with special attention to students with chronic absenteeism. He advocated the organization of "peer calling groups" whose members call one another to encourage school attendance or call a member who is absent. Other instances of systematic accounting systems have been documented for monitoring behavior and homework.

THE CONCEPT IN PRACTICE

In practice, the use of older students to shepherd and guide younger students in the multigrade classroom can enhance the effectiveness of a teacher's classroom management program. In the lab school setting, older students acting as peer mentors are assigned to younger students for the purpose of peer problem mediation and positive peer pressure. Mediating conflicts, misbehavior, and other problems experienced by younger students empowers older students while assisting the teacher with classroom management. Positive peer pressure on younger students through encouragement and prompting of socially accepted behavior provides them with a firm foundation.

TEACHING AND LEARNING

> Providing individualized instruction, requiring subject mastery, implementing cooperative learning, and utilizing computer-assisted instruction are all effective practices in alternative education.

Frank (1984) identified classroom practices that lead to student success. Instructional leadership, teachers who emphasize the basics with effective teaching strategies and evaluation techniques, and educators with high expectations who create a supportive climate in the school are a few of these practices.

Effective teaching and learning strategies include individualizing instruction for the learner, utilizing cooperative learning, and using computer-assisted instruction to enhance learning. An effective evaluation technique is to require content mastery by students in all subjects (Figure 7.4).

Individualized Instruction

Bialo and Sivin (1989) found that alternative programs for at-risk students are typically small, which makes it more realistic and easier to

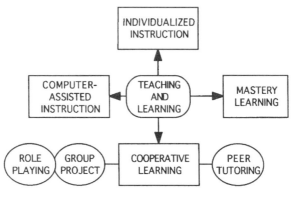

Figure 7.4 *Teaching and learning.*

provide an intimate, supportive climate for students and makes it more likely that the staff will work with students individually. These authors observed that the curriculum tends to be varied, with a mixture of direct instruction and experience-based learning, along with an emphasis on helping students deal with social, economic, and other problems (p. 37).

CONCEPTUAL BACKGROUND

Boyer (1987) contended that class size is crucial for our nation's future. It is simply not enough that teachers give only a minute or two to each child per hour in classes with thirty or more students. Small classes bring more academic gains, increase availability of resources, and enhance the opportunity for individualized instruction.

Cuban (1989) confirmed that small numbers help to foster enduring relationships among adults and students. The potential for students to participate in activities is greater in small programs. Cuban stated, "A class size of 15–20 students permits a level of personalizing instruction unavailable in crowded settings" (p. 30). Harris, Hedman, and Horning (1983) also promoted small classes in the Journey House Program. In the program, classes were usually no larger than twelve to ensure that every participant received the personal attention promised upon entering the program (p. 35).

Klausmeier and Weber (1984) focused on "individual educational programming" as a system for arranging a program of study for each student that meets both the student's needs and legal requirements. They suggest that individual instructional programming be used where instruction is arranged for each student in the classroom, considering the student's aptitudes, interests, motivation, and goals. Klausmeier and Weber contend that students typically require some teacher-directed, small group, and individual activities as part of their planned program (p. 81).

THE CONCEPT IN PRACTICE

The lab school practices individualized instruction using Klausmeier and Weber's "individual instructional programming" format. Each student's aptitudes, interests, and goals are considered when prescribing an affective education program. In turn, students' academic needs and legal requirements are considered when prescribing a cognitive education program. Each student is administered a battery of tests to determine individual needs, aptitudes, and interests for the purpose of individualization. An individualized program of study is then developed and prescribed using prescription cards for each subject area.

In the lab school setting, the use of the U.S. Basics Comprehensive Competencies Program (CCP) affords staffers the assessment instruments and prescription cards for placing learners in individualized instructional programs. Students are placed in courses contained in the U.S. Basics curriculum, a self-paced, competency-based program of study.

Mastery Learning

Through the individualization of instruction determined from pretesting and the use of self-paced, competency-based resources, mastery learning has become an effective practice in science, social studies, math, and English. Mastery learning levels have allowed for more meaningful and consistent teaching, learning, and student evaluation in each of the academic areas.

CONCEPTUAL BACKGROUND

One approach to teaching and learning, called "mastery learning," has been developed by Benjamin Bloom, a noted educational psychologist, and his associates. Bloom's basic message is that even though differences in intelligence and aptitude do exist in every classroom, teachers can adjust the nature of instruction and the time allowed for each student so that more students can succeed (Ryan & Cooper, 1995).

Ryan and Cooper (1995) report that the effects of mastery learning strategies generally seem favorable, particularly in connection with other instructional approaches, such as cooperative learning. The effectiveness of mastery learning is rooted in past problems concerning teaching and learning. Ryan and Cooper described the major problem researched by Bloom as follows:

> Most students are provided with the same instruction in terms of amount, quality, and time available for learning. When this occurs, students who possess more aptitude for given subjects will outperform students possessing less aptitude. But if one accepts that students are normally distributed according to aptitude, one can match the kind and quantity of instruction and the amount of time available for learning to the characteristics and needs of each student. Then the majority of students may be expected to achieve mastery of the subject, and hence the name "mastery learning." (p. 337)

THE CONCEPT IN PRACTICE

In practice, mastery learning programs are effective with alternative school students who need a different approach to learning than is offered by the typical regular school. In the lab school setting, students assigned an individualized instructional program participate in mastery learning as a strategy for dealing with individual differences. Each student, regardless of differences, is provided with the opportunity for self-paced, repeated learning until mastery of subject matter is achieved. This strategy is instituted for each of the four major subjects: math, social studies, science, and English. Students continually restudy and retest until all learning objectives have been mastered.

Cooperative Learning

In a country beginning to question the extent of individualism among its citizens, Ryan and Cooper (1995) saw cooperative learning strategies are a welcome addition to education. "In addition to the moral values of tolerance and concern for others that are fostered through this methodology, it produces greater achievement, particularly in students who are typically low achievers. Students who are usually behind in class, find it much less threatening to take instruction from other students than from teachers" (Ryan & Cooper, 1995, p.278). Thus, peer tutoring programs, group projects, and role playing are effective methods of peers instructing peers in cooperative settings.

PEER TUTORING

Braddock and McPartland (1990) advocated extra help by teachers for any student having serious difficulties in the classroom. According to these authors, the use of peer tutoring within the regular school schedule can prevent course failures.

Conceptual Background

Hamby (1989) advocated the development of peer tutoring programs in alternative schools, noting that "at-risk students can serve as tutors, as well as being tutored by other students" (p. 23). Jenkins and Jenkins (1987) found that "Peer tutoring produced more than twice as much achievement as did computer-assisted instruction, three times more than reducing class size . . . and close to four times greater achievement than would result from lengthening the school day by one hour" (p. 65).

The Concept in Practice

In practice, peer tutoring consists of students helping students because they have some skill or knowledge that others can benefit from. In the lab school setting, older students are matched with younger students based on compatibility for the purpose of assisting them with subject matter. Others are placed in teams of four students per cooperative learning group for essentially the same purpose, but on a larger more cooperative scale. In either case, peer tutors seem to receive a self-esteem boost from their newfound leadership and responsibility, while those being tutored or aided by participation in a cooperative learning group gain academically and socially from the experience.

Computer-Assisted Instruction

Hancock (1993) found that the use of technology affirms students' strengths and accelerates performance outcomes. Hancock concluded that at-risk youngsters need the benefits and high support that carefully planned technology programs can provide them. Technology offers students learning resources that complement and enhance their ability to learn.

CONCEPTUAL BACKGROUND

Bialo and Sivin (1989) contended that computers can provide a multisensory approach to learning, an alternative to traditional instructional arproaches with which at-risk students may have experienced failure. The computer can also provide an instructional sequence that is tailored to the needs of the individual student. Computer-assisted instruction can help change the way students feel about themselves, one another, and their teachers. In addition, the computer can provide students with a sense of academic privacy, especially in a lab setting where students work independently. In the computerized classroom or lab, teachers can spend their time helping, explaining, and prompting students, relating to them as individuals.

Gross (1989) described computer-assisted instruction (CAI) as based on sound learning theory and validated by records of student progress that do not add extra work for teachers. Gross found that computer-assisted instruction keeps youngsters in school. Further, students who devote a short period of time each day to reading and math will graduate with sufficient skills to enter the world of work. With skills development virtually guaranteed by a CAI system, teachers and students are freed to expand on the creative, mind-stretching, and interpersonal experiences that make life worth living.

According to Pogrow (1990), computers offer several advantages in education, such as their ability to mix visual, tactile, and listening modalities, so students can learn through whatever modality they prefer. Computers also provide a private environment in which students can test their ideas at their own pace, out of the public eye. Last, the immediate feedback that computers give enables students to test their ideas and engage in thinking about the computer's reaction. Pogrow concludes:

> Computers thus provide a great vehicle for developing creative and sophisticated curriculums and pedagogical practices. But we have to stop viewing computers as deliverers of instruction. . . . We must all, in short, combine our points of view if we are to best apply the power to technology, new theories of cognition, and learning traditions from other disciplines,

cultures, and art forms. And we must recognize that a roundabout but sophisticated approach to using technology may improve the learning of at-risk students much more than direct but simplistic routes. (p. 65)

THE CONCEPT IN PRACTICE

In practice, computer-assisted instruction is an effective method of enrichment or instructional enhancement for alternative education students. In the lab school setting, students are provided with computer-assisted instruction when the print curriculum needs reinforcing or when students are having difficulty understanding subject matter. The U.S. Basics Comprehensive Competency Program provides instructional software correlated with print material for easy access by students in need of instructional reinforcement, enhancement, or enrichment. The lab school utilizes this curricular program due to its comprehensive instructional methods and formats. Computer-assisted instruction is most effective when utilized in unison with print materials, supplementary reading materials, and multimedia materials. All of these formats are provided by the U.S. Basics Corporation.

STUDENT EVALUATION

Setting an 80% mastery level, retesting until achievement, requiring a work portfolio in the affective areas, and participating in instruction are all effective practices in alternative education.

Conceptual Background

Glasser (1992) contended that all teachers embrace the traditional method of evaluating student progress, a method of evaluation that no more than half of the students handle successfully. Glasser portrayed our present method of evaluation as consisting of both quantity and quality. In other words, Glasser described quality schools as those that evaluate based on all students doing competent work plus some work that is quality work. In addition, all students have a chance to learn without time constraints. Examples of alternative evaluation methods cited by Glasser involve no failure, self-paced learning, self-evaluation, striving for quality, demonstration of competence or mastery when ready, working together, getting credit for accomplishments, and having an opportunity for improvement and grade enhancement.

In the spirit of Glasser's "competence plus quality" concept of evaluation, Figure 7.5 shows a variety of methods for evaluating students. Formatively evaluating students based on 80% mastery of objectives, testing and retesting until formative mastery and summative gains are achieved, using portfolio completion to evaluate affective skills, and evaluating students based on participation in instruction are all effective methods.

Mastery Level

As a means of formatively evaluating the progress of students throughout the school year, this author set an objective mastery level of 80% for attainment of learning objectives in the lab school setting. The mastery level may vary due to the circumstances of a given program, but the same general principles apply. Students not reaching the objective mastery level after initial evaluation are required to continue work on the objectives in question until mastery is attained, whereas students attaining lesson mastery are allowed to move to the next lesson. The process

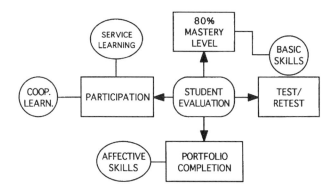

Figure 7.5 *Student evaluation.*

repeats itself until unit mastery is attained, and eventually subject mastery becomes a consideration.

Test/Retest

Students can be tested and retested both formatively and summatively while in alternative education. During the course of instruction in the lab school setting, students are tested frequently to verify formative mastery of learning objectives designed as a result of pretesting. After course mastery has been declared through formative means of evaluation, final posttests are administered to determine benchmark gains in skill level. Posttesting in the lab school setting usually occurs at the conclusion of a semester or school year. An alternate form of the Test of Adult Basic Education (TABE) is administered to students and test results from both forms are compared.

Portfolio Completion

"Along with book bags and lunch boxes, many students now tote something new to school, portfolios of their work. The use of portfolios is becoming increasingly popular in U.S. schools as teachers look for alternatives to traditional tests to measure student progress" (Black, 1993, p. 44).

According to Black (1993), "portfolios are one answer in the search for alternative ways to assess students' performance . . . portfolios are supposed to show what students have learned and what their abilities are according to researchers Lorraine Valdez Pierce and J. Michael O'Malley." In her writings, Black provided selected research defining what is meant by portfolios:

> Judith Arter defines a portfolio as "a purposeful collection of student work that exhibits to the student and others effort, progress, or achievement in a given area or areas." F. Leon Paulson and Pearl R. Paulson emphasize process over product in their defintion: "A portfolio is a carefully crafted portrait of what someone knows or can do."(p. 44)

Teachers may find someone else's definition suitable, or they may choose to write their own. In any case, Black recommends that educators consider appropriate standards for judging portfolio materials, determining what should be included, and how to store portfolios, and communicating results to parents and policy makers.

This author is using portfolio development in the lab school setting as a formative means of evaluating students in their affective education courses. Portfolio development is the perfect method for providing students an opportunity for self-assessment, personal insight, and exploration. Students are able to use their creativity and self-expression to communicate what they learned and how it applies to their lives. Students are required to develop a portfolio of personal journal writings, reports on issues affecting their lives, experiences in their service learning program, descriptive responses to questions concerning their identified risk areas, and assignments relating to specific areas of affective education. Students are required to develop a portfolio throughout the semester in question, with evaluation occurring formatively during each of three grading periods.

In the lab school setting, formative evaluation of a student's work portfolio entails assessment of progress toward its development. Summative evaluation of portfolios, on the other hand, entails determining if students have completed the content requirements of the portfolio. Additionally, effort, progress, and insight are evaluated, as well as achievement. Instead of traditional grading methods (which still present an unsolved problem area in the world of portfolios), checklists and narratives are used to provide feedback and award credit. Teachers check for completion and provide comments referring to the different sections of the portfolio. Finally, extra effort and creativity are considered when assigning grades or credit to portfolio completion.

Student Participation in Instruction

Through cooperative learning groups and service learning experiences, students can participate directly in their own instruction. Cooperative learning groups provide students with an opportunity to work together, assist each other, and participate in student-centered instruction. At the same time, service learning provides students with a school or community project used as a backdrop for learning the principles of community service and citizenship through direct participation. Both instructional methods afford students an opportunity for instructional planning, self-assessment, and self-evaluation. Additionally, teachers can base evaluation on participation variables instead of solely traditional means.

REFERENCES

Bialo, E. R., & Sivin, J. P. 1989. "Computers and at-risk youth: A partial solution to a complex problem," *Classroom Computer Learning,* 19(5):35–39.

Black, S. 1993. "Portfolio assessment," *The Executive Educator,* 2:44.

Boyer, E. L. 1987. "Early schooling and the nation's future," *Educational Leadership,* 44(6):4–6.

Braddock, H. J., & McPartland, J. M. 1990. "Alternatives to tracking," *Educational Leadership,* 47(7):76–79.

Bronfenbrenner, U. 1986. "Alienation and the four worlds of childhood," *Phi Delta Kappan* (February):430–436.

Cuban, L. 1989. "At-risk students: What teachers and principals can do," *Educational Leadership,* 46(5):29–32.

Dinkmeyer, D. C., Pew, W. L., & Dinkmeyer, D. C., Jr. 1979. *Adlerian Counseling and Psychotherapy.* Monterey, CA: Brooks/Cole, p. 311.

Frank, C. 1984. "Equity for all students: The New York City promotional gates program," *Educational Leadership,* 41(8):62–65.

Glasser, W., M.D. 1992. *The Quality School: Managing Students without Coercion.* New York: Harper Perennial Publishers, pp. 226–236.

Gross, B. 1989. "Can computer-assisted instruction solve the dropout problem?" *Educational Leadership,* 46(5):49–51.

Hamby, J. V. 1989. "How to get an 'A' on your dropout prevention report card," *Educational Leadership,* 46(5):21–28.

Hancock, V. E. 1993. "The at-risk student," *Educational Leadership,* 50(4):84–85.

Harris, J., Hedman, C., & Horning, M. 1983. "Success with high school dropouts," *Educational Leadership,* 40(6):35–36.

Jenkins, J. R., & Jenkins, L. M. 1987. "Making peer tutoring work," *Educational Leadership,* 44(6):64–68.

Klausmeier, H. J., & Weber, L. J. 1984. "Improving secondary education in Wisconsin," *Educational Leadership,* 41(6):80–84.

McLaughlin, T. F., & Vacha, E. F. 1992. "School programs for at-risk children and youth: A review," *Education and Treatment of Children,* 15(3):255–267.

Pogrow, S. 1990. "Socratic approach to using computers with at-risk students," *Educational Leadership,* 47(5):61–66.

Ryan, K. & Cooper, J. M. 1995. *Kaleido Scope: Readings in Education.* Boston, MA: Houghton Mifflin Co., pp. 271–278.

Ryan, K. & Cooper, J. M. 1995. *Those Who Can Teach.* Boston, MA: Houghton Mifflin Co., pp. 130–137.

Short, P. M. 1988. "Planning and developing in-school suspension programs," *Monographs in Education, Vol. 9,* C. T. Holmes (Ed.). Athens, GA: College of Education, University of Georgia.

Wehlage, G. G., Rutter, R. A., & Turnbaugh, A. 1987. "A program model for at-risk high school students," *Educational Leadership,* 44(6):70–73.

SUGGESTED RESOURCES

U.S. Basics, "The Comprehensive Competencies Program," United States Basic Skills Corporation, 1700 Diagonal Road, Suite 400, Alexandria, VA 22314.

Chapter 8

THE IMPLEMENTATION DOMAIN: STUDENT SERVICES

> There is no such thing as a "self-made" man. We are made up of thousands of others. Everyone who has ever done a kind deed for us, or spoken one word of encouragement to us, has entered into the make-up of our character and of our thoughts, as well as our success.
> —*George Matthew Adams*

Many different services have been provided to students in addition to the usual and necessary curricular and instructional offerings typical in general education. Services in the implementation domain found effective with alternative education students include provisions for school-to-work transition, service learning and citizenship, guidance and counseling, student recognition programs, business and community partnerships, and management of disruptive students through reform efforts (Figure 8.1).

SCHOOL-TO-WORK TRANSITION

Emphasizing workplace readiness, career exploration, career and educational planning, and work experiences for at-risk students are effective practices in school-to-work transition.

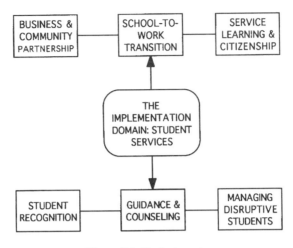

Figure 8.1 Student services.

Most students readily admit that their academic classes are of little use to them in the real world. They feel that history, algebra, literature, and biology are mere stepping stones to a diploma or postsecondary schooling. Most need down-to-earth, relevant experiences that facilitate a smooth transition between school and work. Figure 8.2 charts workplace readiness, career exploration, career and educational planning, and work study as experiences preparing students for a smooth transition between school and the world of work.

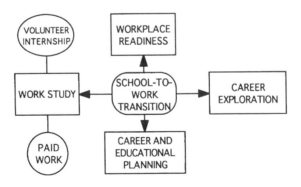

Figure 8.2 School-to-work transition.

Workplace Readiness

Workplace readiness is one variable in the push for effective school-to-work transition of alternative education students. Preparing for the world of work after school completion is an important goal for any successful school-to-work transition program. Alternative education programs need to make school-to-work transition a top priority in their efforts to serve students in more productive ways than afforded by regular schools.

CONCEPTUAL BACKGROUND

Mark Newton, Director of Organizational Development for Cincinnati Gas and Electric, stated, "A workforce that possesses both technical competence and employability skills is no luxury—it's a necessity." In today's changing workplace, technical skills are a must. But career success depends on workers being able to adapt quickly and effectively to new demands and expectations.

What Work Requires of Schools, a SCANS Report for America 2000, identified problem solving, teamwork, and self-management as essential competencies, skills, and personal qualities for all students—both those going directly to work and those planning further education. Paul O'Neill, Chairman of the President's Education Policy Advisory Committee, commented, "This report goes well beyond 'the basics.' It provides a fresh and, above all, realistic look at the new and different kinds of skills and knowledge workers need in today's workplace—and need to be able to adapt to tomorrow's workplace" (Agency for Instructional Technology, 1994, p. 5).

THE CONCEPT IN PRACTICE

In practice, workplace readiness consists of those classroom experiences that prepare students for the world of work. In the lab school setting, workplace readiness coursework is a prerequisite to placement in a work study program. Students receive learning modules featuring various activities, video, computer, and interactive technologies, as well as print material with worksheets and problem-solving workbooks.

The Agency for Instructional Technology provides a complete package, *Workplace Readiness: Education for Employment.* Problem solving, teamwork, and self-management—three units of workplace readiness—are identified as "essential competencies, skills, and personal qualities for students by the SCANS report."

The Agency for Instructional Technology (AIT) is a nonprofit U.S.-Canadian organization established in 1962 to strengthen education. AIT provides leadership and service to the education community through cooperative development, acquisition and distribution of technology-based instructional materials. The agency is headquartered in Bloomington, Indiana.

Career Exploration

Career exploration represents a systematic and planned inquiry and analysis of careers of interest to individual students. Comparisons, reality testing, as well as standardized testing can be helpful in the career exploration process. Classes in career exploration are not uncommon in education today (Gibson & Mitchell, 1986).

CONCEPTUAL BACKGROUND

As mentioned earlier, Isaacson (1985) considered interest inventory results the major means for exploring occupational options, describing several interest inventories that are keyed directly to occupational options. Clients tend to focus attention on interest scores to confirm their subjective evaluations and then move their attention to occupations named by those scores. Interest inventories and the resulting occupational options can help at-risk students identify career goals early in high school, thereby increasing their chances of completing a high school education.

THE CONCEPT IN PRACTICE

In practice, classes are an effective means of providing opportunities for career exploration. In the lab school setting, the *Occupational Outlook Handbook* (1994–1995) is used to study careers through an analysis of the thirteen career clusters. Supplementary materials such as pamphlets, videos, and career software are also used on a regular basis to study career clusters of interest. In addition, the Self-Directed Search by John L. Holland is used with the procedures for exploration followed as outlined in his book, *Making Vocational Choices: A Theory of Vocational Personalities and Work Environments* (Holland, 1985). This combination of resources has been effective in exposing alternative education students to careers of interest or compatibility.

Career and Educational Planning

Awareness of the relationship between educational opportunities and the world of work is an important aspect of career and educational planning. After career exploration, students need to narrow their career or career planning possibilities and then proceed to examine and test these options as critically as possible. An educational program compatible with students' career goals is planned as part of this process.

CONCEPTUAL BACKGROUND

Beck (1991) found that school personnel can be a significant factor in keeping students in school by assisting them with career and educational planning. Beck recommends that counselors coordinate orientation for preemployment awareness, training in life, coping and work readiness skills, and entry into the job market. Successful career programs are characterized by cooperation with business leaders, intensive student counseling, practical work experience, and training in basic skills needed for success on a job.

THE CONCEPT IN PRACTICE

In practice, career and educational planning occurs after career exploration and before job placement in a work study program. In the lab school setting, students are exposed to such established techniques as values clarification, standardized testing, job shadowing, and group guidance. Students learn decision making, including choosing between competing alternatives, examining the consequences of specific choices, recognizing the value of compromise, and implementing a decision. Students are helped to recognize the impact of their current planning and decision making on their future life and are encouraged to become active in shaping their own futures and preparing for the world of work.

Work Study

The work study curriculum consists of two similar components. As described in the following, paid work and volunteer internships are both effective methods for involving youth in the world of work.

PAID WORK

Paid work experiences are those in which the employer provides the student worker with monetary compensation. Monetary compensation may be in addition to school compensation providing students with course credit toward promotion and/or graduation.

Conceptual Background

Mackey and Appleman (1983) found that adolescents are likely to be more attached to their jobs than to school. Therefore, they contend that as work becomes more pervasive in adolescent society, it should be incorporated into the school curriculum. Work experiences for students can become part of the total school program in the form of paid work programs.

The Concept in Practice

In practice, eligible students can be afforded an opportunity for a paid work experience after participating in workplace readiness training, career exploration, and career and educational planning. In the lab school setting, students over the age of fifteen are afforded an opportunity for paid work study. Depending on the number of academic courses required, older students can leave school after lunch to report to work or to prepare for work later in the day. All work study students must participate in a school-to-work class held for one half hour after lunch. Students may find their own job or seek assistance from the school-to-work coordinator for job placement. In either case, students are encouraged to seek employment in a position similar to identified areas of interest or aptitude.

VOLUNTEER INTERNSHIP

Volunteer internships are opportunities for students to gain valuable work experience as trainees in participating businesses, while acting in a service capacity as a volunteer. Interns receive no monetary compensation, but do receive course credit toward grade promotion and/or graduation.

Conceptual Background

Walls (1990) advocated a cooperative partnership between schools and local businesses in an effort to provide work experiences for youth. Young potential employees are supplied to businesses in return for individual attention and future opportunities for entry-level employment to students who might otherwise have dropped out of school. Students are assigned a mentor from the participating business along with an internship in the company. The business gives the students on-the-job training and assists with career exploration. In return, the school system agrees to train the businesses' employees in mentoring skills and help them know what to expect from the students in the program.

The Concept in Practice

In practice, after workplace readiness training, career exploration, and career and educational planning, students under the age of fifteen are placed in a variety of internship positions at participating businesses, government agencies, and corporate industries, related to their identified areas of interest or aptitude.

Students are rotated through several cluster positions during the course of a year as a means of exposing them to different types of work. A student interested in a career in the service industry, for example, can be rotated through different service positions, such as teacher's assistant, day care worker, and nurse's aide. A particular student may rotate to a new position every nine weeks or so, or remain longer in one position classified as a high-interest area.

SERVICE LEARNING

Providing students with civics instruction and program training, a service project, and an opportunity for reflection and expression of learned outcomes are effective practices in service learning.

Advocates view service learning as an important and necessary component in the education of American youth today. What interests those of us involved in dropout prevention is its obvious potential to make a significant difference in the lives of at-risk youth. Academic learning, problem-solving skills, self-esteem, attitudes toward others, and social responsibility are positively affected by a service learning experience. (Duckenfield & Swanson, 1992, p. 21)

In advance of the service learning experience, students receive civic preparation and training in service to others. They are then provided either an indirect service, direct service, or civic action field experience. During the field experience, students have opportunities for reflection through sharing and discussion. Through projects and writing assignments, students are able to express what they have learned from their experience (Figure 8.3).

Preparation: Learning Activities

Preparation consists of the learning activities that take place prior to a student's volunteer work. Students need guidance and support before they are sent out into the school or community to serve. For example, students must understand what is expected of them as well as what they can expect from the service project (Duckenfield & Swanson, 1992).

CIVIC PREPARATION

Preparation for the service learning experience involves assessing community needs and student interests. The experience becomes more meaningful for students if they have been afforded a role in assessment activities, particularly self-assessment.

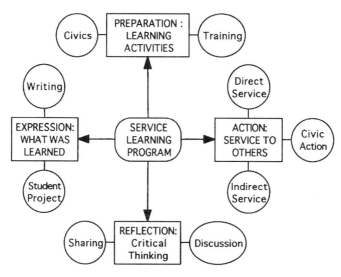

Figure 8.3 *Service learning program.*

Conceptual Background

It is critical that the students themselves be involved in the process of identifying the civic problems and social issues in their community. This can be done by researching the agencies in the community, conducting interviews with community experts, surveying teachers and students, and making site visits to observe civic problems in the community (Duckenfield & Swanson, 1992; Maryland Student Service Alliance, 1989b). "Examples of social issues in which students may choose to become involved include serving the aging, disabled and disadvantaged; preventing crime, substance abuse, and teenage pregnancy; and saving the environment" (Duckenfield & Swanson, 1992, p. 13).

The Concept in Practice

In practice, after completing the necessary civic preparations, students select a project area of interest. In the lab school setting, selections are based on students' findings during community and self-assessment. Students are given time to brainstorm ideas for projects and problem solving. For example, students must consider where they wish to serve, how much time it will take, and what type of resources will be needed to complete the project.

TRAINING

An effective service learning program includes a well-planned system for training students. Such training ensures that the students get the most from their service experience and contribute the most to their community (Duckenfield & Swanson, 1992; National Crime Prevention Council, 1988).

Conceptual Background

Service training occurs in a variety of settings such as a classroom course, a student retreat, a series of workshops, or a single meeting. Student motivation and interest is facilitated through role plays, initiative games, video presentations, guest speakers, and assigned research topics. Training consists of service orientation, skill building, and followup and closure procedures (Boyce & Cairn, 1991; Duckenfield & Swanson, 1992).

According to Boyce and Cairn (1991), orientation provides students with the opportunity to ask questions and explore experiences and issues that they may encounter during their service. In addition, certain skills may need to be acquired before actual participation (Duckenfield & Swanson, 1992). These skills may consist of general service skills, hands-on techniques, and technical skills. Lastly, closure helps participants formally deal with the issues that surface when a service relationship is over.

The Concept in Practice

In practice, the training orientation is used to introduce students to the people with whom they will be working and the procedures and responsibilities that will be involved. Skill building includes learning cooperation, communication, organization, responsibility, problem solving, and awareness of working with special populations (Duckenfield & Swanson, 1992).

In the lab school setting, training is ongoing throughout the service project. Followup occurs regularly until the project ends and closure becomes necessary. Closure helps participants deal with issues that surfaced throughout the service experience.

Action: Service to Others

Action is the actual caring for others performed by the student participating in the service project. The service itself must be engaging, challenging, and meaningful. The action phase is a time when adjustments to the initial service plan may be made in response to conditions and circumstances (Maryland Student Service Alliance, 1989b).

Students can participate in service activities through direct service, indirect service, and civic action, as described in the following.

DIRECT SERVICE

Students can choose to participate in service learning activities through direct service to others. Students chosing direct service generally feel comfortable working in close proximity with others.

Conceptual Background

According to Duckenfield and Swanson (1992), "Direct service requires personal contact with people in need. This type of service is generally the most rewarding for students because they receive immediate positive feedback during the process of helping others" (p. 14).

"Whenever possible, students should be encouraged to commit to direct service projects that last for several weeks or months. This gives students time to feel they have made a contribution, to develop friendships with the people they are serving and serving with, and to understand better the problem they are working to solve" (Maryland Student Service Alliance, 1989b, p. 14).

The Concept in Practice

In practice, direct service to others requires the student participant to work in close proximity to people in need. In the lab school setting, alternative education students work in a variety of school-based service projects. Older students are assigned to younger students as peer tutors and peer mentors in the alternative school. Others are assigned to local elementary schools as mentors and teacher assistants in the lower grades. Still others work individually with the small children of teen parents while the parents attend classes.

During the course of this important service project, a related need was discovered: staffers taking toddlers outside to a neighboring playground for recess were having difficulty supervising and attending to each child. As a result, a group of male alternative education students decided to make supervision of these children a new service learning project. The project required each teen to pair with a toddler in a shepherding situation for the purpose of supervision, facilitation of play, and individual mentoring. The toddlers are safer, engaged, and benefitting from one-on-one attention from a male significant other. Service providers take their work very seriously and conduct it with great pride.

INDIRECT SERVICE

Students can also participate in service learning activities through indirect service to others. Students choosing this option generally prefer channeling their personal resources to a particular problem that does not involve direct contact with others.

Conceptual Background

Indirect service activities are easily organized and involve channeling resources to the problem rather than working directly with an individual who may need service. This type of service may be of the least value to students because they are so far removed from the need and do not directly experience the benefit of their efforts (Duckenfield & Swanson, 1992; Maryland Student Service Alliance, 1989b).

The Concept in Practice

In practice, the value of indirect service is usually diminished because students are removed from the root of the problem or need and, therefore, do not realize the direct benefit of their efforts. In the lab school setting, indirect service projects have been developed that are based on alternative program needs and problems. Using school-based problems and needs reverses the "diminished benefits" trend to a certain extent. Students can better understand the need for clerical, secretarial, and custodial services in their own school after learning that support and resources for alternative education are usually limited and better diverted to teachers and material resources. Since the students themselves are the beneficiaries of funds and resources diverted from these support positions, the rationale for indirect service projects becomes much clearer. Students volunteer for projects that include answering the school's phones, staffing the reception area, caring for the grounds, cleaning the building, assisting with lunch service, filing papers, making copies, and working as teacher assistants. As a result, the need for support personnel is diminished and funds are used for other more direct support positions.

CIVIC ACTION

Students can also choose to participate in service learning activities through civic action projects. Students choosing this type of service want to directly impact their community by working to eliminate the causes of a specific problem.

Conceptual Background

Civic action is a third type of service activity directly related to good citizenship. According to the Maryland Student Service Alliance (1989b),

> Civic action involves working to eliminate the causes of a specific problem and to inform the public about the issues surrounding that problem. Students may petition local government . . . or they may initiate a campaign to bring about public awareness. Young people are very effective in bringing about political change, especially when they feel truly committed to the cause. (p. 15)

The Concept in Practice

In practice, civic action involves working towards resolution of a community problem by trying to alleviate its causes. In the lab school setting, students are trying to reverse the decline of a deteriorating neighborhood by cleaning up lots and parks within its boundaries. Students can take pride in the fact that the neighborhood is where their school is located. This type of project creates a common bond between its residents and alternative education students.

Another civic project is a recycling program taken on by students after realizing the need for community recycling. The hub of recycling efforts takes place within the confines of the alternative school and transfers to a broader community focus.

Reflection and Expression

Reflection and expression is the component that enables students to think critically about their service experiences and share them with others, thereby providing a structured opportunity for students to learn from their experiences. It involves observation, questioning, and putting new ideas together to add meaning to the service experience (Conrad & Hedin, 1987; Duckenfield & Swanson, 1992).

Duckenfield and Swanson (1992) identified several principles characteristic of quality reflection:

> For significant learning and effective service to occur, reflection must be well structured and have clear objectives. Activities can be well planned yet flexible enough to allow learning to happen spontaneously. Quality reflection must be an interactive, interesting and an ongoing process. Students are involved in reflection throughout the service experience, from beginning to end. (p. 15)

Duckenfield and Swanson found that a major purpose of school-based service learning is to transfer service learning to the school curriculum. Classroom reflection and expression are facilitated through the curriculum through the discussion, sharing, writing, and various student developed projects.

DISCUSSION AND SHARING

Students can engage in a discussion and time of sharing about their service learning experience with a group of other service participants. This time of reflection is an important step in the process of understanding the meaning of service to others.

Conceptual Background

Discussion and sharing involves groups of students talking about the personal meaning of their service experience. Discussion and sharing is stimulated through the presentation of a brief statement or reading related to the service in which the student is engaged. This method allows participants to focus on particular issues in service learning, examining what has been said about the issues they are now confronting. Readings in the service area encourage students to discuss their reactions with group members and set the stage for further inquiry and action (Maryland Student Service Alliance, 1989a).

The Concept in Practice

In the lab school setting, students are first divided into groups with participants in similar service project areas. In essence, this leads to three different groups: direct service, indirect service, and civic action. These groups discuss and share similar, different, and unique experiences within their particular areas. Later, groups are changed to mix students with participants in other service learning project areas, which affords students an opportunity to gain exposure to service projects in completely different areas. Such exposure may lead students to try a different type of service experience in the future.

WRITING ASSIGNMENTS AND STUDENT PROJECTS

Writing is a natural outgrowth of discussion and sharing. Projects, on the other hand, are developed by students to raise their awareness about issues associated with service. Both methods are effective in expressing what was learned through the service experience and the followup time of reflection (Duckenfield & Swanson, 1992).

Conceptual Background

Duckenfield and Swanson (1992) described writing assignments as including letters, essays, stories, newspapers, and journals. They found journal writing to be an excellent way for students to explore their service experience on a very personal level. Journal writing enables students to think about the results of their experience, and causes them to gain personal insights and discover how they relate to others.

Duckenfield and Swanson (1992) found that many methods can be employed to highlight the service area, ranging from posters, plays, and multimedia presentations to research. Learning becomes more meaningful, however, when students create their own projects. Students can do interviews, documentaries, and personal videos as a means of creating a personal project.

The Concept in Practice

In practice, writing assignments and student projects follow discussions and times of sharing as reflection and expression activities. In the lab school setting, students keep ongoing personal journals about their service experience. Throughout the service project, students make regular entries in their journals, and use them as references when participating in reflection activities.

Students must also complete a summary of their service experience once it has been completed. The journal becomes a very important resource when developing this summary. In addition, students are given the opportunity to complete a project about their service experience for presentation to other service learning participants. Students can research their topic at the local library and add their personal experiences to their findings. The resulting presentation is conducted in front of the class as a culminating experience.

GUIDANCE AND COUNSELING

> Providing students with regular group guidance, as well as individual, group, and academic counseling are all effective practices in guidance and counseling.

Figure 8.4 depicts suggested guidance and counseling initiatives for alternative education programs. Activities include daily group guidance and individual counseling initiatives, small-group counseling activities, and academic counseling. All make up a comprehensive guidance and counseling service necessary for effective alternative education programs.

Daily Group Guidance

Group guidance is one component of a comprehensive guidance and

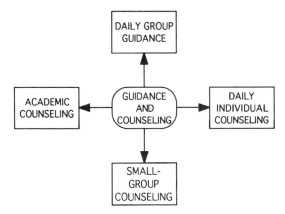

Figure 8.4 *Guidance and counseling.*

counseling program. Providing all students with daily group guidance on topics covering a wide range of social/emotional issues is an effective practice in alternative education.

CONCEPTUAL BACKGROUND

Positive school guidance experiences must negate the discouragement and alienation most alternative school students have acquired through their previous formal education. Educators must promote personal and social development in students through these types of experiences. Now, unfavorable conditions in the home, church, and community require the schools to intervene in this manner through guiding social development and positive citizenship in young people (Wehlage, Rutter, & Turn-baugh, 1987). Wehlage et al. concluded that a healthy society is tied to disadvantaged students gaining the skills and attitudes that will make them productive workers as well as effective parents and good citizens. These goals can be accomplished through a well-thought-out group guidance program facilitated by teachers or counselors.

THE CONCEPT IN PRACTICE

In practice, students benefit from meaningful group guidance provided on a regular basis. In the lab school setting, students receive daily classroom guidance through the life skills and personal development curricula on issues ranging from self-esteem to conflict resolution. Teachers, counselors, or guest presenters facilitate group guidance activities within the classroom setting. Group guidance is a program requirement in addition to students' regular academic coursework.

Daily Individual Counseling

Individual counseling is the second component of a comprehensive guidance and counseling program. Providing daily opportunities for individual counseling when needed is an effective practice in alternative education.

CONCEPTUAL BACKGROUND

Cardenas and First (1985) promoted the strengthening of counseling services for non-college-bound youth and the development of counseling programs for at-risk students. In addition, they recommended that a comprehensive individual career counseling program be available for all youth. This is particularly necessary for students opting or mandated to attend alternative school programs.

Yaffe (1982) advocated beginning dropout prevention efforts with individual counseling. Since counseling can help stop problems before they become chronic, personal counseling is considered an important element in all alternative programs.

THE CONCEPT IN PRACTICE

In practice, students benefit from individual counseling on a regular basis. In the lab school setting, time is set aside daily for individual counseling. Types of individual counseling range from personal problem resolution to career counseling.

Small-Group Counseling

Small-group counseling is the third component of a comprehensive guidance and counseling program. Providing students experiencing common problems with regular small-group counseling is an effective practice in alternative education.

CONCEPTUAL BACKGROUND

Ogden and Germinario (1988) aimed at bringing together students with similar academic, behavior, and family related problems. Such close-knit groups may help students better understand the nature of their dysfunctional feelings and behaviors, and provide a basis for social support among students. Small-group counseling should be facilitated by trained guidance counselors or alternative educators trained in group dynamics (p. 57).

THE CONCEPT IN PRACTICE

In practice, small-group counseling should be carried out regularly with students experiencing common problems. In the lab school setting, various types of counseling groups are developed and offered to students identified as experiencing the particular problem being addressed in the group. For example, a group designed for students who are chronically behind in grade is held on a weekly basis as a means of addressing problems related to this issue. Additionally, a group for students affiliated with gangs is held regularly as a means of addressing common problems associated with gang activity.

Academic Counseling

According to Beck (1991), one of the most effective strategies for helping an at-risk student is one-to-one involvement with an advisor or counselor in a helping, caring environment. Teachers-as-counselors encourage the student to finish school and plan for the future. Further, mentoring programs can use school personnel to provide extra help in subjects and reinforce study skills and life skills.

CONCEPTUAL BACKGROUND

Braddock and McPartland (1990) contended that teachers should provide extra help to any student having serious difficulties. For example, within the regular school schedule, coaching sessions could help educators intervene in the course failures of students (p. 77). Slavin, Karweit, and Wasik (1993) found that out of all the strategies they reviewed, the most effective for preventing failure used one-to-one tutoring of at-risk students. They reported that although immediate outcomes for all forms of tutoring were very positive, the most impressive effects have been found for programs that use teachers as tutors (p. 14).

Wehlage, Rutter, Smith, Lesko, and Fernandez (1989) advocated an "extended role" for teachers in dealing with the whole child. They stated:

> This means that teachers must be willing to deal with certain problems in the home, community, or peer group to promote student success in school. For example, the teacher may need to confront a substance abuse problem . . . if a student is to learn and develop. (p. 71)

This extended role puts the teacher in the position of advisor for the students needing advisement, guidance, and support.

Keefe (1986) summarized a method of improving teacher-student relationships through "personalization." That is, "The advisors in this system are responsible for contacting persons concerned with the student with information and feedback about progress in school. During the diagnosis of the student, the advisor becomes aware of the student's learning history and characteristics" (p. 33–34).

Scardamaglia (1993) described a program in which teachers were given released time to become advocates for students labeled at-risk. The teachers worked with students who needed extra attention or a trusted friend to talk to. According to Scardamaglia, student advocates are not intended to take the place of the regular school counselor, although they do receive training in intervention techniques. The advocate's role is simply to be an effective mentor.

THE CONCEPT IN PRACTICE

As a result of the concepts discussed above, the term "academic counselor" has taken root as a practice in alternative education. Teachers acting in the capacity of academic counselor in the lab school setting have helped at-risk students reduce their disruptive school behavior while improving school achievement, self-confidence, and attendance.

STUDENT RECOGNITION

> Awarding students for academic mastery, good attendance and behavior, and overall improvement through a luncheon where students receive various gifts and privileges is an effective practice in student recognition.

Conceptual Background

Wager (1993) found that a system of rewards for students could reinforce a system of prohibitions and punishments. Thus, strong incentives combined with strong disincentives could dramatically influence children's behavior and also win the cooperation of parents. Similarly, Hamby (1989) promoted the recognition of improvement as well as absolute achievement by expanding honor rolls, sending letters to parents, and awarding ribbons. Hamby also promoted the use of objective measures in determining these rewards in order to eliminate the possibility of bias.

Ogden and Germinario (1988) recommended using recognized payoffs for students as they meet the expectations of the school. Recognizing subject mastery, behavior and attendance, and most improved students is important to maintaining a learning climate. All children must be given the opportunity to be rewarded, preferably during a special event, as a means of fostering positive attitudes (Figure 8.5).

SUBJECT MASTERY CERTIFICATES

In the lab school setting, certificates are awarded for subject mastery in each of the academic disciplines. Each subject area teacher awards students at each grade level certificates for subject mastery and high

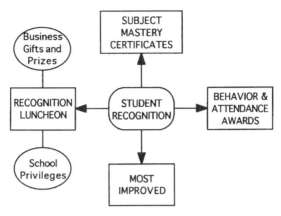

Figure 8.5 *Student recognition.*

achievement. Certificates are given for achievement in mathematics, science, social studies, and English, as well as enrichment and remedial courses.

BEHAVIOR AND ATTENDANCE AWARDS

Students in the lab school setting are awarded behavior and attendance certificates for good performance. Each six-week report card period is used to award these certificates. Students are awarded for best behavior and perfect attendance. If no student has perfect attendance, then the student with the best attendance receives the certificate.

MOST IMPROVED STUDENT AWARD

Students in the lab school setting compete for the "Most Improved Student Award." Criteria for the award are based on improved academic performance, behavior, attendance, and attitude. Each six-week report card period provides students with a new opportunity to earn this award.

RECOGNITION LUNCHEON

Students in the lab school setting compete for a spot among the "Super

Six" during each six-week report card period. The "Super Six" students attend an all-you-can-eat recognition luncheon at a local restaurant where they are honored for their achievements. The "Super Six" have exhibited exemplary academic achievement, behavior, attendance, and attitude during the course of the report card period.

BUSINESS AND COMMUNITY PARTNERSHIPS

Securing adopt-a-school sponsors, staffing for an inter-agency center, mentors from the business and community sectors, and volunteer staff members are all effective practices in business and community partnerships.

Bucci and Reitzammer (1992) emphasized that the schools must establish relationships with community groups and health and social service agencies to help students address their problems. Adults from local colleges, senior citizen centers, businesses, and community groups are usually willing to work with the local school system and individual students. "Schools should reach out to these groups and individuals to make them feel welcome" (Bucci & Reitzammer, 1992, p. 67). Schools can reach out to these groups through adopt-a-school programs, inter-agency centers, business mentoring programs, and volunteer programs as charted in Figure 8.6.

Hamby (1989) advocated fostering communication between parties as a first step in increasing awareness of the dropout problem among students, parents, and community leaders. Educators should communicate often with these groups about their school-related programs. Cooperating with business and industry to publicize the importance of staying in school is equally important.

Ramirez (1990) stated, "Parents, lawmakers, business leaders, and others in the community must support a school system's efforts to serve dropouts and troubled teens" (p. 24). For dropouts, Ramirez believed support services were as important as instruction. He contended that a program should consider students' physical, economic, social, emotional, and academic needs.

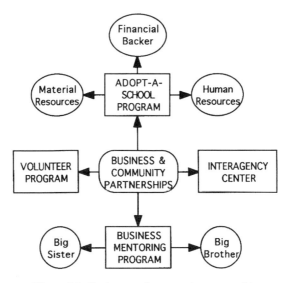

Figure 8.6 *Business and community partnerships.*

Adopt-a-School Program

Adopt-a-school program partners can be utilized in several ways depending on the particular needs of the alternative education program. For example, sponsoring businesses can provide financial backing, human resources, or material resources for the program in question. In any case, adopt-a-school partners serve in a support capacity for their adopted alternative education program.

CONCEPTUAL BACKGROUND

Walls (1990) found that indicators of a successful alternative program included utilizing a support system, strengthening ties with community organizations, and coordinating school services. Walls advocated forming partnerships with local businesses and assigning each student a mentor and a job with the sponsoring business. In return, the school system would agree to train the participating business employees in mentoring skills and help them learn what to expect from the students in the program. In addition, sponsoring businesses could offer financial, human, and material resources to participating schools.

THE CONCEPT IN PRACTICE

In practice, business sponsors can be of any variety and type so long as they are willing to offer support to the alternative education program. The lab school utilizes several different types of business partners in their adopt-a-school program, each with a different purpose. For example, a local school supply store acts as a provider of material resources to the program. A group of local grocery stores provide jobs for alternative education students, whereas local law enforcement provides mentors. Lastly, a local rental housing business provides financial support by purchasing "wish list" items for staff members and students. Each sponsor provides a specific type of service to the program, some by design because of the type of business engaged in.

Interagency Center

Cuban (1989) advocated coordinating at-risk programs with an array of social services that students need, such as mental health, Department of Family and Children Services, psychological services, and court services. To this end, Cuban suggested that the teacher, adviser, or special staff member make linkages with social services, and that the pressing needs of each student be dealt with by people knowledgeable about each particular child's background.

CONCEPTUAL BACKGROUND

Clough (1990) described how student assistance programs, both preventive and interventive, are able to garner individual counselors, school nurses, and community agencies for use with at-risk students. These resources assist in gathering information on at-risk students and facilitating the problem-solving effort by responding to specific problems in their area of expertise.

Mitchell and Johnson (1986) suggested a cooperative approach to serving at-risk youth that involved pooling staff and resources from several contributing agencies providing comprehensive diagnostic assessments and treatment planning services. The cooperative approach was created out of a need to coordinate services for at-risk youth. According to Mitchell and Johnson, the best chance of making a difference in the lives of children lies in coordination of resources and cooperative intervention (p. 62).

THE CONCEPT IN PRACTICE

In practice, agency collaboration with alternative school personnel for the purpose of providing services to students usually takes place through school visitation by caseworkers from the various agencies. In the lab school setting, this concept has been taken a step further. An on-site interagency center is staffed by full-time caseworkers from four different agencies: Juvenile Court, Department of Family and Children Services, Mental Health, and Vocational Rehabilitation. Alternative education students, as well as students from around the school system, benefit from these school-based social services.

Caseworkers are "repositioned" from agencies to the school-based center for the purpose of providing direct services to students. The accessibility of human and material resources is significantly enhanced by the presence of on-site caseworkers. This type of arrangement is made possible through the development of partnerships and the pooling of resources by the school system and agencies in question.

Business Mentoring Program

Smink (1990) found that mentors from the business world forge a valuable link with the school of which the student is the beneficiary.

CONCEPTUAL BACKGROUND

A mentoring program provides individualized interaction that is normally impossible for teachers and administrators to provide due to large classes and high student-teacher ratios. A mentor is interested in the personal as well as the academic growth of the student—something educators have difficulty finding time to do. In addition, educators are struggling with a high failure and dropout rate of better than 25 percent. These at-risk students often have the greatest need for mentoring due to their low self-esteem and history of failure (Smink, 1990).

THE CONCEPT IN PRACTICE

In practice, mentoring is not utilized to its greatest potential in many school systems. In the lab school, however, mentors are assigned to individual students willing to participate in the mentoring program. Mentors act as shepherds to their assigned students, providing them with tutoring, field trips, and work experience, or simply luncheons together at local restaurants. Mentors also track student progress, shadow students between home and school, and monitor attendance. Mentors are free to visit the school at any time during the day for the purpose of mentoring. Mentors are considered an extension of the alternative school staff because of the valuable service they provide to students. For this reason, mentors are referred to as "big brothers" and "big sisters" by the alternative staff.

Volunteer Program

In this era of limited resources and financial cutbacks, volunteers have become a valuable commodity in alternative education. Thus, the use of volunteer staff reduces the pupil-staff ratio, while providing alternative programs with additional resources and services.

CONCEPTUAL BACKGROUND

Hamby (1989) promoted the use of volunteers as tutors at all grade levels as a means of assisting with students at-risk. Hamby recommended that volunteer tutors include parents, senior citizens, high school students, college students, business persons, and anyone else with the interest and skills to help (p. 23).

THE CONCEPT IN PRACTICE

In practice, volunteerism is a cost-efficient method of providing resources and services to students. In the lab school setting, volunteers serve as teacher assistants in classrooms, clerical staff in the office, and custodial help with the school plant. Volunteers are also used to monitor the hallways and greet visitors to the school. Volunteerism is a critical component of the alternative education program.

HELPING CHRONICALLY TROUBLED STUDENTS REFORM

> Helping students clarify their problem area, participate in self-esteem building, and work through reform to elicit change are effective practices with troubled students.

Before chronically troubled students can begin the reform process, they must be willing to make the necessary changes. As charted in Figure 8.7, chronically troubled students must first clarify their problem area if change is to occur. Clarification of a problem area begins when the student's behavioral history is identified as either disruptive, rebellious, aggressive or criminal, or a combination. With assistance from a counselor, mentor, or other staff member, students can further clarify their

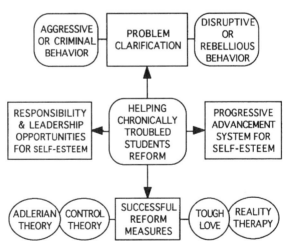

Figure 8.7 *Helping chronically troubled students reform.*

problem area by becoming familiar with the characteristics of their identified behavior area and the causes behind them.

Low self-esteem is the main reason behind the inappropriate behavior of troubled students. The causes of low self-esteem can often be traced to a variety of events and circumstances ocurring throughout the troubled student's family, social, and personal life. Reversing sometimes years of "self-esteem battering" is not easy. Often it takes a variety of positive experiences over a period of time to make a difference. One such experience is the use of a "progressive advancement system" in the alternative education setting. Another is the provision of responsibility and leadership opportunities for students. Both have been used effectively with the chronically troubled student.

Problem clarification and improvement in self-esteem alone do not result in reform of the chronically troubled student, however, in order to elicit real, long-lasting results, ongoing therapeutic program should be standard practice with troubled students in alternative education programs. Some effective reform measures drawn from the literature are the concepts pertaining to Adlerian theory, control theory, Toughlove, and reality therapy. These practices, and others, have proven successful with troubled students in a variety of settings, including alternative education programs.

Problem Clarification

Clarifying students' problem areas involves identifying them as either disruptive, rebellious, aggressive, or criminal. Further, many students are characterized as exhibiting multiple behavior types, such as disruptive and rebellious or aggressive and criminal. Chronic disruptive students often exhibit specific characteristics from all four types of behavior. These are the students who are often referred to as "out of control" by both school and community officials. Students not chronically troubled by definition are usually classified by their reason for enrollment, such as dropout recovery, pregnancy or birth, or other reasons of choice.

CONCEPTUAL BACKGROUND

The Georgia Department of Education (1994) uses several categories to characterize chronically troubled students enrolling in their Crossroads alternative education programs. These categories are defined below:

- disruptive behavior: behavior other than physical aggression that disrupts the learning of other students or the student himself, such as verbal aggression, arriving late to class, or behavior that distracts the attention of the teacher or the other students
- rebellious behavior: behavior that rebels against school rules, such as refusing to do assigned work, skipping school, smoking, leaving campus without permission, coming to school under the influence of drugs or alcohol, or not following rules regarding private cars
- aggressive behavior: behavior that demonstrates physical aggression, such as fighting, striking or pushing a student or teacher
- illegal behavior: behavior that is against the law, such as carrying a weapon to school, possessing, selling or using drugs or alcohol at school, theft, vandalism, etc.

THE CONCEPT IN PRACTICE

In practice, chronically troubled students can be characterized upon enrollment as either disruptive, rebellious, aggressive, criminal, or a combination of one or more of these areas. In the lab school setting, students receive affective learning packets in each area of characterization. Some students have several learning packets in their portfolio because several problem areas have been identified. The more negative behaviors identified, the more packets assigned to a student's portfolio. Students are required to complete work on each learning packet before progressing through the student advancement system discussed in the following.

Packet completion entails reading and analyzing information, role plays, and definitions pertaining to the particular area being studied. Students must answer questions over the reading material before packets are considered complete. Once a student completes the portfolio of learning packets, he or she is eligible for advancement to the next level in the system.

The lab school uses the *Discipline Advantage Learning Packet System* developed by Advantage Press, Incorporated. This system consists of several varieties of specific and general packets at two different levels. Both the high-school and middle-school versions include two or more sets of questions in each topic area. Examples of topic areas include Late to School, Cut Class, Unprepared for Class, Disturbed Class, Disrespectful Behavior, Away from Assigned Area, and Problems with Relationships. General topics include Uncooperative Attitude, Learning from Mistakes, and Taking Suggestions. Packet order forms can be requested by writing: The Advantage Press, Incorporated, 2731 Maple Avenue, Post Office Box 1405, Lisle, Illinois 60532.

Progressive Advancement System for Self-Esteem

The progressive advancement system is an effective classroom prevention/intervention strategy that utilizes a sequential progression of promotional stages with built-in privileges at each level. Attainment of the highest level usually indicates achievement of predetermined goals, such as grade promotion or return to the regular school environment.

CONCEPTUAL BACKGROUND

According to Hefner-Packer (1991), low self-esteem is the predominant characteristic of at-risk students. Successful learning situations in a personalized environment help improve self-esteem, positively influencing student approaches to problem solving. Hefner-Packer found that the self-image of alternative school students appears to improve, especially for those who have not done well in traditional schools. Specifically, alternative school students tend to develop better attitudes toward school, seem to gain an increased sense of control over their destinies, and demonstrate a stronger self-identity when returning to the regular school.

THE CONCEPT IN PRACTICE

In order to provide a personalized environment conducive to successful learning experiences as advocated by Hefner-Packer, a "progressive advancement system" has been devised and practiced by this author for the promotion of self-esteem in students. This organizational scheme contains four promotional levels: entry, adjustment, model, and return.

As students progress through the four sequential levels, responsibility, leadership opportunities, and privileges begin to increase.

The entry level begins when a student enters the program, and no special privileges are attached. The adjustment level begins as soon as a student has satisfied all entry requirements and has been placed in a classroom. Adjustment level students begin earning their way academically and behaviorally to the next level, resulting in an opportunity for special privileges, increased responsibility, and leadership. Upon reaching the model level, students begin to receive privileges, responsibility, and leadership opportunities modeled after those granted in the regular school. Students are expected to "model" regular school behavior to avoid demotion to a lower level. Lastly, students promoted to the return level are eligible for reintegration in their home school if their progress is maintained. Students failing to maintain return level standards face demotion to a lower level.

Self-esteem is impacted when students begin achieving success at each of the different levels in the system. For example, increasing privileges, responsibility, and leadership roles tend to create positive change in participating students, facilitating feelings of self-worth and a desire to "move up the ladder." Of course, these are characteristics directly transferable to the world of work and life in general.

Responsibility and Leadership Opportunities for Self-Esteem

Edgar (1989) contended that "A student's self-esteem is an important link to academic and social success. . . . A program needs to be long term in duration since once a child's self-esteem has been negatively affected. . . . Many successes are required to help a child feel better about himself" (p. 37). Any program must concentrate on eliminating the student's attitude towards failure acceptance.

CONCEPTUAL BACKGROUND

Emmerich (1983) posited that educators should include leadership training at the secondary level by offering training programs for youth. Such programs would include lectures, discussions, and small-group experiential activities along with self-assessment. Participants can also use a professionally published instrument that determines behavioral patterns and provides feedback on their value and effectiveness in groups. Students can view videotapes of themselves, receive feedback from their peers and teachers, and critique their own leadership techniques.

Kenney (1987) described a peer leadership approach in which young people role play, meet with fellow students, answer their questions, distribute literature, and make referrals to community agencies as a means of assistance. According to Kenney, teens tend to listen to their peers and, with accurate information, can have a significant impact on others.

Emmerich (1983) found that as a result of training, trainees experience positive relationships with adult leaders, greater self-esteem, and encouragement for the future. Trainees can also expand their social circles across cultural and economic levels and develop resource networks among their peers (p. 65).

Hamby (1989) suggested the involvement of students in school clubs as a way to increase their self-esteem. Such involvement gives students the opportunity to come up with innovative ways to solve problems responsibly and help the community.

George and Mooney (1986) described the Miami Boys Club Delinquency Prevention Program as an innovative and successful approach to reform through education and counseling (p. 78). This school club, which runs a reform program targeted at hard-core male delinquents, operates as follows:

> At the end of the regular school day, the student is met by his counselor and transported to the Boys Club for an afternoon of academic instruction, counseling, and recreation. The Boys Club program begins with a nutritious snack followed by two hours of tutoring in mathematics and language arts. Following tutorial instruction, the boys engage in team and individual games, and receive counseling. (p. 77)

George and Mooney concluded, "Students . . . have shown dramatic reductions in criminal activity, sharply reduced rates of absenteeism from school, and a significant improvement in grades. . . . Academic placement has also improved by one grade level or more after one year in the program"(p. 77).

THE CONCEPT IN PRACTICE

If you give alternative education students leadership opportunities, you have given them responsibility. This philosophy was adopted by this author when putting the concept of responsibility and leadership into practice. Students first received leadership training through a series of group forums, lectures, and weekend retreats designed for teenagers. In addition, during the school year, these students were provided with a variety of leadership opportunities. One such opportunity, the practice of placing students in kindergarten classrooms as teacher assistants, was particularly effective. With an opportunity for high-level responsibility in such an important leadership position, alternative education students experienced unprecedented self-esteem gains. A major part of these gains can be attributed to the added benefit of a position in which teenagers receive constant love and approval from admiring children, something rarely experienced from members of their own peer group. Consequently, leadership opportunities involving working with peers or independently of others do not lead to gains in self-esteem as quickly. Three practices of this type effectively impact self-esteem, however, the use of older students as peer mentors, peer tutors, and office assistants.

Effective Reform Measures

Out of the many prepackaged programs available for therapeutic assistance with at-risk students, most are patterned after a particular philosophy. Repeatedly, the same theorists, particularly from the human development and counseling schools of thought, are cited as the source behind many of the life skills and personal development programs on the market. Four such theories: Adlerian, control, Toughlove, and reality, are tailor-made for working with the chronically troubled student. Each postulates that the only way to break the cycle of chronic misbehavior and acting out is for staff members to take the initiative and stop the punishment. Only through treating hard-core discipline problems with much less coercion can we make a difference. This is easy to say, but difficult to do. It can only be accomplished by a staff who understands control theory and Toughlove, and is willing to practice reality therapy and Adlerian counseling.

ADLERIAN THEORY

Approaches to helping troubled children based on the individual psychology of Alfred Adler promote discipline as the development of personal responsibility and suggest that educators and parents nurture this responsibility in children. Meanwhile, educators and parents should come to a better understanding of the reasons why children misbehave as a way to guide a child's behavioral development so that he or she can function effectively throughout life.

Conceptual Background

Adlerians view each person, even the youngest child in the family, as an individual who has the creative capacities to decide and choose. The actions of each person, therefore, are purposeful, indivisible, and socially based. One of the basic premises of Adlerian theory is that we are primarily social beings and that our behavior occurs in a social context (Dinkmeyer, Pew, & Dinkmeyer, 1979).

According to Adler, all human behavior has a purpose. Simply stated, Adlerians think that we understand people and their behavior best in terms of their goals. Therefore, goal-directedness is probably the most important explanation of behavior and misbehavior (Dinkmeyer, Pew, & Dinkmeyer, 1979).

Dreikurs (1968) wrote that the goal-directed nature of behavior can perhaps be best understood in terms of the goals of misbehavior. Dreikurs classified all child misbehavior into four categories that are still relevant today, each corresponding to the goal of the misbehavior: attention, power, revenge, and display of inadequacy. Dreikurs noted that there may be other ways in which teenagers can find their place in a destructive way, through sexual experimentation, smoking, drug and alcohol abuse, gang membership, and other means of excitement. Certainly, this has been found to be true almost thirty years later.

Although the solutions proposed over the years have varied, the approaches based on the individual psychology of Alfred Adler promote discipline as the development of personal responsibility and natural consequences as a replacement for rewards and punishments. Instead of reacting punitively or permissively, parents and educators are urged to come to a better understanding of the reasons why children misbehave in order to assist them with behavioral planning. Practitioners such as Dreikurs, Dinkmeyer, Pew, and Dinkmeyer, Jr., have taken Adlerian theory and applied these concepts in a practical way to the educational setting.

The Concept in Practice

This author instituted reform practices for troubled students in the lab school setting based on Adlerian concepts. The first practice mandated that administrators and counselors consult with teachers and parents about a particular student's discipline problems. Administrators and counselors were not content to deal with the observed behavior alone, but tried to understand the purpose of the student's behavior. Staff members felt that only if they were able to understand the child's mistaken behavior would they be able to cooperatively plan with the student helpful approaches to reform.

The second practice mandated that the administrator or counselor try to bring about a general agreement among the parents, the school personnel, and the student concerning the best course of action. The administrator and/or counselor acted as a consultant to teachers and parents concerning the basic principles of Adlerian theory and how to apply them.

The third practice, learning the skills of encouragement and consistency and the use of natural and logical consequences, was used in developing a course of action and behavior plan for the future. Using natural and logical consequences instead of rewards and punishments effectively helped students assume responsibility for their actions and behavior, a mainstay in Adlerian theory. Staff members found that when students have something at stake when deciding to act, they often choose carefully and wisely.

CONTROL THEORY

Control theory is a new and powerful explanation of how we behave. It explains why far too many capable students make little or no effort to learn. Glasser (1986) warned that we are mistaken if we believe that discipline, dropouts, and drugs are what is wrong with the schools of today. Glasser contends that through learning-teams, the classroom teacher can begin to solve the real problem, lack of effort.

Conceptual Background

According to control theory (Glasser, 1992), all human beings are born with five basic needs built into their genetic structure: survival, love, power, fun, and freedom. Consequently, life is spent attempting to satisfy one or more of these needs. Glasser found that we try to control our own behavior so that what we choose to do is need-satisfying. Clearly, much of what we choose to do is an attempt to control others. "Control theory, therefore, is the explanation of this constant attempt to control both ourselves and others, even though in practice we can control only ourselves" (Glasser, 1992, pp. 43–44).

> From birth, our behavior is always our best attempt at the time to do what we believe will best satisfy one or more of our needs . . . we spend our lives trying to learn how to satisfy these needs, but most of us do not have a clear idea of what they are . . . what we know, however, is how we feel . . . and what we actually struggle for all of our lives is to feel good. (Glasser, 1992, p. 44)

It is through these feelings that most students gain an idea of what their needs are.

In his book, *Control Theory in the Classroom,* Glasser (1986) strongly suggested that students be taught in cooperative groups during their academic classes. Learning together as members of a small learning team has been found to be much more need-satisfying, especially for the needs of power and belonging. Students seem to learn more and have fun doing it. Glasser found that good teachers recognize that when they can promote and support worker cooperation, they have laid the foundation for quality work and needs satisfaction.

The Concept in Practice

"A good school could be defined as a place where almost all students believe that if they do some work, they will be able to satisfy their needs enough so that it makes sense to keep working" (Glasser, 1986, p. 15). With this definition in mind, the concepts of control theory were put into practice in the lab school setting. First, teachers were exposed to the basic concepts of control theory so that they could put them into practice with their students. Second, by exposing teachers to control theory in the lab school setting, they were able to teach the concepts to their students. In turn, students were better able to help themselves when getting into trouble instead of taking up the time of a counselor or administrator.

In keeping with the concepts of control theory, students were assigned to small groups in their classrooms. Not only were students learning their academics in the cooperative group setting, they also learned about control theory. Staff members felt that if this was the recommended learning format for academic classes, students would excel by learning control theory from these same groups. Further, this practice gave teachers an opportunity to observe and work with students in the group setting before having to fully implement the concepts in the academic setting.

Participating teachers found that student misbehavior declined when they felt their needs were being met. By working with others cooperatively, achieving success academically, and possessing the skills to control their own behavior, students found school much more fulfilling.

TOUGHLOVE

When parents and teachers can't reach troubled teens, it's time for Toughlove. Ann Landers stated, "Toughlove teaches you to face the crisis, take a stand, demand cooperation, and meet challenges" (York, York, & Wachtel, 1982). The use of Toughlove is an effective practice in helping chronically troubled students reform.

Conceptual Background

Toughlove is a solution to the problem of unacceptable behavior among young people. Supporting parents, encouraging cooperation in the adult community, and making young people who act out accountable for their behavior in a cooperative environment comprise the fundamental activities of Toughlove (York et al., 1982).

Toughlove is difficult from the standpoint that adults must act differently than they ever have before. However, Toughlove is also loving. Toughlove is not nasty, abusive, or vindictive. Instead, Toughlove means standing firm, knowing what plan to follow to deal with destructive behavior, and loving students enough to do what has to be done, no matter how hard you find the task, for example, when you must go to the police to turn in a student or expel a student for repeated misbehavior. York et al. (1982) contend that this is precisely what makes Toughlove so tough.

The Concept in Practice

Upon implementing a Toughlove mentality in the lab school setting, staff members found that it was exactly what was needed to respond to chronically troubled students. The difficult steps that parents and teachers must take in responding correctively to unruly teenagers are exactly what Toughlove prescribes. Therefore, Toughlove seems to be a perfect match for alternative education. Furthermore, Toughlove provides the added benefit of involving parents. Parents benefit from the skills Toughlove teaches. Thus, parents learned skills, attitudes, and strategies for helping them with their unruly children at home, while teachers learned similar skills for working with these children in the alternative classroom.

REALITY THERAPY

Another intervention theory that has gained popularity in recent decades is reality therapy, largely developed by William Glasser (Gibson & Mitchell, 1986). From a reality therapy standpoint, "counseling is simply a special kind of teaching or training that attempts to teach an individual what he should have learned during normal growth in a rather short period of time" (p. 118).

Conceptual Background

Glasser (1984) suggested that reality therapy "focuses on the present and upon getting people to understand that they choose essentially all their actions in an attempt to fulfill basic needs. . . . The therapist's task is to lead them toward better or more responsible choices that are almost always available" (p. 320).

Thus, reality therapy focuses on present behavior and does not emphasize a student's past history. It is based on the assumption that the student will assume responsibility for his or her well-being. Proponents of reality therapy praise students when they act responsibly and express disapproval when they do not (Gibson & Mitchell, 1986).

Corey (1977) summarized the reality approach as "an active, directive, didactic, cognitive behavior-oriented therapy. The contract method is often used, and when the contract is fulfilled, therapy is terminated. The approach can be both supportive and confrontational. 'What' and 'how,' but not 'why' questions are used" (p. 49).

The Concept in Practice

Through my use of reality therapy in the lab school setting, I can declare without reservation that it has direct implications for situations in alternative education. Gibson and Mitchell made the connection between reality therapy and alternative education when they said, "counseling is simply a special kind of teaching or training that attempts to teach an individual what he should have learned during normal growth in a rather short period of time" (p. 118). This one phrase has implications for alternative educators everywhere, since most serve students with normal growth deficiencies in alternative placement for a short period of time.

REFERENCES

The Advantage Press, Inc. 1988. *Discipline Advantage Learning Packet System.* Lisle, IL: Author.

Agency for Instructional Technology. 1994. *Workplace Readiness: Education for Employment.* Bloomington, IN: AIT.

Beck, M. S. 1991. "Increasing school completion: Strategies that work," *Monographs in Education , Vol. 13,* C. T. Holmes (Ed.). Athens, GA: College of Education, University of Georgia.

Boyce, K., & Cairn, R. W. 1991. "Orientation and training," *The Generator,* 11(3):6.

Braddock, H. J., & McPartland, J. M. 1990. "Alternatives to tracking," *Educational Leadership,* 47(7):76–79.

Bucci, J. A., & Reitzammer, A. F. 1992. "Teachers make the critical difference in dropout prevention," *The Educational Forum,* 57:63–69.

Cardenas, J., & First, J. M. 1985. "Children at risk," *Educational Leadership,* 43(1):4–8.

Clough, G. 1990. "Student assistance program screening: Matching needs with resources," *Adolescent Counselor,* 42(4):38–39, 53.

Conrad, D., & Hedin, D. 1987. *Youth Service: A Guidebook for Developing and Operating Effective Programs.* Washington, DC: Independent Sector.

Conrad, D., & Hedin, D. 1991. "School-based community service: What we know from research and theory," *Phi Delta Kappan,* 72(10):743–749.

Corey, G. 1977. *Theory and Practice of Counseling and Psychotherapy.* Monterey, CA: Brooks/Cole.

Dinkmeyer, D. C., Pew, W. L., & Dinkmeyer, D. C., Jr. 1979. *Adlerian Counseling and Psychotherapy.* Monterey, CA: Brooks/Cole, p. 311.

Dreikurs, R. 1968. *Psychology in the Classroom.* New York: Harper & Row.

Duckenfield, M., & Swanson, L. 1992. *Service Learning: Meeting the Needs of Youth at Risk.* Clemson, SC: National Dropout Prevention Center.

Edgar, S. 1989. "An analysis of the effects of an intervention program on academic, social, and personal adjustment of at-risk and retained seventh and eighth grade students" (Doctoral dissertation, Northern Arizona University, 1987), *Dissertation Abstracts International,* 49:7920A.

Emmerich, M. 1983. "Training tomorrow's leaders today," *Educational Leadership,* 40(6):64–65.

George, P., & Mooney, P. 1986. "The Miami Boys Club delinquency prevention program," *Educational Leadership,* 43(4):76–78.

Georgia Department of Education. 1994. *Crossroads Interim/Annual Report.* Atlanta, GA: Division of Research, Evaluation and Assessment.

Gibson, R. L., & Mitchell, M. H. 1986. *Introduction to Counseling and Guidance.* New York: Macmillan Publishing Company.

Glasser, W. 1984. "Reality therapy," in *Current Psychotherapies* (3rd ed.). R. J. Corsini (Ed.). Itasca, IL: F. E. Peacock, pp. 320–353.

Glasser, W., M.D. 1986. *Control Theory in the Classroom.* New York: Harper and Row, Publishers, pp. 7-16.

Glasser, W., M.D. 1992. *The Quality School: Managing Students without Coercion.* New York: Harper Perennial Publishers, pp. 39–57.

Hamby, J. V. 1989. "How to get an 'A' on your dropout prevention report card," *Educational Leadership,* 46(5):21–28.

Hefner-Packer, R. 1991. "Alternative education programs: A prescription for success," *Monographs in Education, Vol. 12,* C. T. Holmes (Ed.). Athens: GA: College of Education, University of Georgia.

Holland, J. L. 1985. *Making Vocational Choices: A Theory of Vocational Personalities and Work Environments.* Englewood Cliffs, NJ: Prentice Hall.

Isaacson, L. E. 1985. *Basics of Career Counseling.* Boston, MA: Allyn & Bacon, Inc.

Keefe, J. W. 1986. "Advisement programs: Improving teacher-student relationships, school climate," *NASSP Bulletin,* 69(489):85–89.

Kenney, A. M. 1987. "Teen pregnancy: An issue for schools," *Phi Delta Kappan,* 68:728–736.

Mackey, J., & Appleman, D. 1983. "The growth of adolescent apathy," *Educational Leadership,* 40(6):30–33.

Maryland Student Service Alliance. 1989a. *Courage to Care, The Strength to Serve: Reflections on Community Service.* Annapolis, MD: CZM Press.

Maryland Student Service Alliance. 1989b. *Draft Instructional Framework in Community Service.* Baltimore: Maryland State Department of Education.

Mitchell, S. T., & Johnson, P. H. 1986. "Richmond's response to students at risk," *Educational Leadership,* 43(5):62–64.

National Crime Prevention Council. 1988. *Reaching Out: School-Based Community Service Programs.* Washington, DC: Author.

Ogden, E. H., & Germinario, V. 1988. *The At-Risk Student: Answers for Educators.* Lancaster, PA: Technomic Publishing Company, Inc.

Ramirez, A. 1990. "These are the hallmarks of effective dropout programs," *The Executive Educator,* 12:23–25.

Scardamaglia, R. 1993. "Teachers as student advocates," *Educational Leadership,* 50(4):31.

Slavin, R. E., Karweit, N. L., & Wasik, B. A. 1993. "Preventing early school failure: What works?" *Educational Leadership,* 50(4):10–17.

Smink, J. 1990. *Mentoring Programs for At-Risk Youth.* Clemson, SC: Clemson University, National Dropout Prevention Center.

United States Department of Labor. 1994–1995. *Occupational Outlook Handbook.* Washington, DC: U.S. Government Printing Office.

Wager, B. R. 1993. "No more suspension: Creating a shared ethical culture," *Educational Leadership,* 50(4):34–37.

Walls, M. W. 1990. "The promise of a job keeps dropout-prone kids in school," *The Executive Educator,* 12(4):22–23.

Wehlage, G. G., Rutter, R. A., & Turnbaugh, A. 1987. "A program model for at-risk high school students," *Educational Leadership,* 44(6):70–73.

Wehlage, G. G., Rutter, R. A., Smith, G. A., Lesko, N., & Fernandez, R. R. 1989. *Reducing the Risk: Schools as Communities of Support.* New York: The Falmer Press.

Yaffe, E. 1982. "More sacred than motherhood," *Phi Delta Kappan,* 63:123–130.

York, P., York, D., & Wachtel, T. 1982. *TOUGHLOVE.* New York: Bantam Books, pp. 149–169.

SUGGESTED READING

Glasser, W., M.D. 1986. *Control Theory in the Classroom.* New York: Harper and Row, Publishers, pp. 7–16.

Glasser, W., M.D. 1992. *The Quality School: Managing Students without Coercion.* New York: Harper Perennial Publishers, pp. 39–57.

Windell, J. 1994. *8 Weeks to a Well-Behaved Child: A Failsafe Program for Toddlers Through Teens.* New York: Macmillan Publishing Company.

York, P., York, D., & Wachtel, T. 1982. *TOUGHLOVE.* New York: Bantam Books, pp. 149–169.

Youngs, B. B. 1991. *How to Develop Self-Esteem in Your Child: 6 Vital Ingredients.* New York: Fawcett Columbine Publishers.

Chapter 9

THE EVALUATION DOMAIN

When possible make the decisions now, even if action is in the future. A reviewed decision usually is better than one reached at the last moment.

—*William B. Given, Jr.*

Comprehensive evaluation of a program, including staff performance and student progress, results in a snapshot revealing the overall picture of alternative education in a particular school system.

Figure 9.1 shows the three types of evaluation critical in alternative education: staff evaluation, program evaluation, and student evaluation. All three provide a comprehensive picture of alternative education using a variety of stakeholders in the evaluative process. A well-rounded program utilizes data from all three sources for the purpose of evaluating effectiveness, strategic planning, and seeking outside funding sources. The remainder of this chapter discusses the three types of evaluation, creating a link between each for the purpose of comprehensive evaluation.

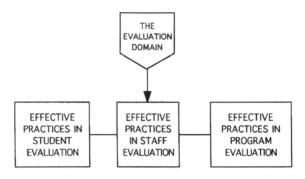

Figure 9.1 The evaluation domain.

EFFECTIVE PRACTICES IN STAFF EVALUATION

Modifying the staff evaluation process and observation instrument is an effective practice in alternative education. The curricular, instructional, support, and managerial practices of alternative educators are typically different from those used by regular educators.

Due to differences in the curricular, instructional, support, and managerial practices of alternative educators, modifications in the staff evaluation process and observation instrument are becoming a necessity. Modifications may be found in the following areas of teacher evaluation: curricular development, provisions for instruction, classroom management, and assessment of student progress (Figure 9.2).

A modified instrument for both formal and informal teacher evaluation is available from Appendix G, Worksheets X and XI.

Modified Curriculum Development

Many alternative education programs are designed to serve students ranging from grades 6–12, concurrently enrolling from several different regular schools. Unfortunately, most alternative programs operate on minimal budgets and rely on outside funding to supplement what they receive from their local school systems. This combination, along with the need to provide students with different methods and materials than those afforded by traditional schooling, has created interesting challenges.

One such challenge is curricular development. How do alternative educators provide their students with an extended curriculum using different methods and materials while meeting minimal state curricular requirements for each grade level? Furthermore, if successful, how do they contend with teacher evaluation processes and classroom observation requirements designed for teachers in traditional settings using traditional methods and materials?

CONCEPTUAL BACKGROUND

According to Ryan (1993), the formal curriculum is usually thought of as the school's planned educational experiences. Ryan contends that our formal curriculum is a vehicle to help young people come to know the good through stories, historical figures, and events. In addition to the formal curriculum, students learn from a hidden curriculum consisting of all the personal and social instruction that they acquire from their day-to-day schooling. The hidden curriculum has been found in some cases to lead to students' loss of self-esteem, obedience to silly rules, and suppression of their individuality. However, many of education's most profound and positive teachings can be conveyed in the hidden curriculum. Therefore, the hidden curriculum must be considered with the same seriousness as the written, formal curriculum. Character education and

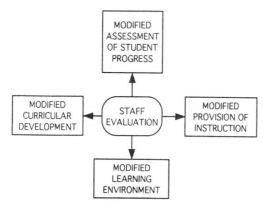

Figure 9.2 *Staff evaluation.*

service to others, for example, are central curriculum issues confronting educators. "Rather than the latest fad, it is a school's oldest mission" (Ryan, 1993, p. 18).

Glasser (1992) warned that it is necessary to recognize that a majority of students believe that much of the present academic curriculum is not worth the effort it takes to learn it. For example, students are asked to learn innumerable facts that both they and their teachers know are of no use to anyone except to pass tests. "While it is not nonsense to ask students to be aware of formulas, dates, and places and to know where to find them if they need them, it becomes nonsense when we ask students to memorize this information and to lower their grades if they fail to do this precisely" (p. 226).

Glasser (1992) emphasized skills, not facts or information when developing a curriculum. Thus, there should be a constant attempt to relate all that is taught to the lives of the students. Beyond skills, Glasser believed that students should be asked to demonstrate that they can use what they have learned. "We should never forget that people, not curriculum, are the desired outcome. . . . What we want are students who have the skills to become active contributors to their society, enthusiastic about what they have learned and aware of how learning can be of use to them in the future" (p. 232).

THE CONCEPT IN PRACTICE

Teachers in the lab school setting have the freedom to be innovative and creative when it comes to curriculum development. More importantly, this freedom has been extended in an environment free from the dreaded staff evaluation process. Of course, there are still requirements for the teaching of English, science, social studies, mathematics, and physical education at each grade level, but the manner in which these subjects are taught and the materials used is evaluated on an individual basis. In addition, teachers have incorporated life skills into these major subjects, as well as the so-called "hidden curriculum," in an effort to instill values, morals, character, civics, and personal living skills in students while continuing to meet subject requirements. Finally, teachers have proven that content area reading and writing is an effective strategy for teaching social studies or science while providing extra language arts instruction.

Utilization of these modified principles of curriculum development run counter to certain aspects of traditional teacher evaluation processes. The Institute of Effective Practices sees a real need for a modified evaluation process and observation instrument, beginning with evaluation of curriculum development in the alternative education classroom. Of course, the need for modifications may vary depending on the characteristics of the alternative education program in question.

Modified Provision of Instruction

Most alternative educators practice nontraditional methods of instruction on a consistent basis. Although alternative educators generate instruction directly from time to time, most instruction is student-generated in the nontraditional classroom. As a result, the focus on transfer of learning moves to the student-generated learning environment. Both student-generated instruction and transfer of learning highlight the need for modifications in the provision of instruction.

CONCEPTUAL BACKGROUND

Ryan and Cooper (1995) noted that Carl Rogers, a counselor, psychologist, and therapist, "used the term facilitator, rather than teacher, because he believed it emphasizes what happens to the learners rather than the performance of the teacher. The term facilitator also implies significantly different functions than does the term teacher" (p. 44). One function involves facilitating on-task behavior and self-paced learning during student-generated instruction. Another requires facilitation of cooperative group work and interactive learning. A facilitator encourages students to make things happen in the learning environment instead of relying on teacher performance.

Students learn by having opportunities to practice and apply new skills or concepts. Rosenshine and Stevens (1986) promoted cooperative groups as a setting in which to practice and apply these newly learned skills and concepts. For group learning to be optimally effective, teachers generally select members who are compatible with each other. Members participate in group activities, some of which are drill and practice, group reviews, team events, and project development. Rosenshine and Stevens emphasize that the advantage of such cooperative settings comes from the social value of working in groups and the cognitive value gained from sharing with others.

New material must be processed in order to be transferred from short-term to long-term memory (Rosenshine & Stevens, 1986). Linking new activities to the students' prior experiences helps elicit transfer of learning (Kounin, 1970). Familiar material is more easily transferred to long-term memory than unfamiliar material. Consequently, Rosenshine and Stevens advocate the processing of new information by making connections between old and new material.

THE CONCEPT IN PRACTICE

Modifications of instruction in a nontraditional learning environment include individualization, self-paced learning, and student-generated instruction with or without teacher facilitation. Student-generated instruction is carried out using a variety of strategies. Evaluation in the lab school setting called on teachers to assume the role of facilitator, allowing students to generate their own instructional experiences with the guidance of the teacher. Student-generated instruction is enhanced through opportunities for content linked to relevant life experiences, prior or future learning, or through associations. Such opportunities make learning more interesting and provide for transfer of learning despite the lack of teacher-generated instruction.

Modified Classroom Management

Alternative educators' classroom management techniques are usually different from those used in traditional classrooms. Modifications in methods and strategies are necessary due to the characteristics of the clientele served, objectives of the program, and philosophy of staff members. Observation of classroom management includes evaluating the organizational structure, the physical setting, and teachers' behavior management techniques.

CONCEPTUAL BACKGROUND

Time on task is increased and time for routine tasks is decreased when instructional time is maximized by the teacher. Effective teachers keep the students' environment focused and relatively free of disruptions. Keeping students continuously engaged can be accomplished by providing a sufficient number of activities and sufficient time for each activity.

Efficient transitions between activities also maximize instruction (Hawley & Rosenholtz, 1984). "Students can also share in the responsibility for making smooth transitions by adhering to well-defined rules and playing specific roles during classroom changes" (Levin & Long, 1981, p. 12).

"Arrangements of physical space and seating patterns should complement the teacher's instructional objectives and methods and seek to maximized both the physical space and available resources. Effective teachers organize classrooms with specific, well-equipped areas to accommodate different types of learning activities" (Brophy, 1983; Georgia Department of Education, 1993; Hawley & Rosenholtz, 1984). Ensuring free classroom movement, minimizing crowding, and providing good visual seating through efficient classroom arrangements optimizes instructional opportunities for students.

Undesirable classroom behavior can be prevented through effective use of positive feedback and by modeling desirable behaviors (Cummings, 1980). Classroom managers need to communicate high expectations and hold students responsible for meeting them throughout the school year. Rules should be taught and monitored by the classroom manager. In order to be effective, rules must be clear and reasonable, and fairly and equitably enforced (Hawley & Rosenholtz, 1984).

"Although it is more desirable to prevent misbehavior than it is to have to deal with it once it occurs, all teachers, at one time or another, will be faced with inappropriate behavior that must be addressed" (Cummings, 1980; Georgia Department of Education, 1993, p. 60). Rinne (1984) classified teacher intervention strategies as low-profile, mid-profile, or high-profile responses to student misbehavior. "Whatever strategy is used, however, feedback should be specific and swift; and the consequences should be fair, appropriate, and consistantly applied" (Cummings, 1980; Georgia Department of Education, 1993, p. 60).

THE CONCEPT IN PRACTICE

Modified evaluation of classroom management in the lab school setting calls for constant monitoring of the behavior of class members, providing positive feeback on appropriate behavior, and redirecting when necessary. Teachers are charged with the responsibility of optimizing on-task behavior in an effort to minimize disruptive behavior in the classroom. This author believes that the more actively engaged students are, the less likely they are to misbehave. The focus during classroom observations was on preventing behavioral problems before they occur and intervening in those problem situations that were unavoidable.

Modified Assessment of Student Progress

According to the Georgia Department of Education (1993), evaluation of teachers with respect to student progress should be carried out in four different areas: engagement of students, monitoring of progress, student performance, and support of students. With minimal modifications, these categories are just as effective when evaluating alternative educators as they are with regular educators.

CONCEPTUAL BACKGROUND

Presentations that include something new and exciting maintain students' attention, thereby helping to keep them accountable for learning and engaged in the learning activity (Brophy, 1982; Georgia Department of Education, 1993; Kounin, 1970). "One particular method for promoting engagement is asking for student responses and then using extended teacher wait-time. Wait-time is defined as the length of the pause preceding any teacher utterance" (Georgia Department of Education, 1993, p. 42).

There are many ways to monitor students' progress, including asking strategic questions, interpreting relevant observable behavior during assessing activities, circulating among students during seatwork or individual work times, and asking all students to signal responses (Georgia Department of Education, 1993; Hunter, 1982). Monitoring student progress should take place frequently so that the teacher can provide corrections and reteach when necessary (Rosenshine, 1983).

A major teaching function involves responding to student answers and correcting student errors. By articulating the steps used to arrive at the correct answer, the teacher helps both those students who are still learning the steps in a process and those who need the information to correct errors and understand why the answer was correct (Georgia Department of Education, 1993, p. 46; Rosenshine, 1983).

The Georgia Department of Education (1993) contends that students are affected by their learning environment. Just as a negative climate inhibits student productivity, a positive classroom climate contributes to productivity and achievement. Berliner (1984) notes that "the communication of academic expectations for achievement; development of a safe, orderly and academically focused environment for work; quick, fair and sensible management of deviancy; and the development of cooperative environments for learning contribute significantly to a supportive classroom climate" (pp. 65–66).

THE CONCEPT IN PRACTICE

Evaluation of teachers in the lab school setting focuses on facilitation of engagement either through promotion of on-task behavior during classroom monitoring, through interactive learning using technology and multimedia, or through a variety of strategies, including cooperative group involvement, role playing, etc. Student progress is monitored by interpreting either relevant student responses, contributions, performances, or products such as assessment of mastery learning levels, portfolio development, personal interaction, contributions to cooperative learning groups, or graded work. Students also receive reinforcement for adequate performances and feedback or correctives for inadequate performances. Support for students is conveyed through encouragement, lowering concern levels, dignifying responses, and by avoiding sarcasm, ridicule, and humiliating references.

This author has found that the Georgia evaluation model is most effective with alternative educators in the areas of student progress. With minimal modifications, the indicators for student progress can be fairly applied to the process of evaluating alternative educators.

EFFECTIVE PRACTICES IN PROGRAM EVALUATION

> Using demographic information, as well as input from students, staff members, and the collaborative team for program evaluation are effective practices in alternative education.

According to Hefner-Packer (1991), "Program evaluation is the method of gathering information that supports the decision to continue, modify, or discontinue a program" (p. 41). Evaluation should be conducted on the formative happenings and summative outcomes of program activities. Formative evaluation seeks to determine whether program goals and objectives are being achieved and whether any modifications are required. Summative evaluation, in turn, compares desired outcomes with actual outcomes. According to Hefner-Packer, the primary concern of summative evaluation in alternative education is, "Does the program have a positive impact on children?" (p. 42).

Figure 9.3 displays a variety of stakeholders and the use of demographic information for the formative and summative evaluation of alternative education programs. The collaborative team, students, and staff members can all be involved, to some extent, in the evaluation process.

Using Demographic Information

Gathering a variety of data pertaining to the characteristics of students, staff members, and the program in general provides alternative educators with one means of measuring program effectiveness. Informational data can be collected on students' family, social, personal, and academic background to assist in determining program makeup and its impact on the community.

This author collected demographic data about students in each lab

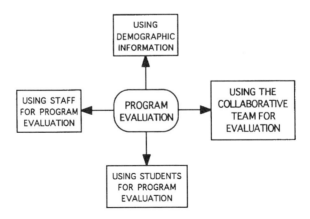

Figure 9.3 Program evaluation.

school classroom at the beginning of the school year and again at the end of the school year. Demographic data were based on the goals and objectives of the program, and measured change, improvement, and outcome variables, as well as any discrepancies between collection periods. The availability of demographic data allowed for an objective evaluation of the program in advance of the more subjective measures involving students, staff, and the collaborative.

A reproducible form for demographic program evaluation is available from Appendix I, Worksheet XII.

Using the Collaborative Team for Evaluation

The collaborative team charged with overseeing and governing the alternative education program can serve as a participant in program evaluation. With the variety of school, community, business, agency, and government representatives typical of effective collaboratives, this team is a natural for evaluating program effectiveness.

Each team member rates or checks the alternative education program on such variables as level of compliance with program assurances, program planning, program development, program implementation, and program management. The collaborative team then makes a written report to the school district with feedback and recommendations for improvement.

A reproducible form for collaborative evaluation of programs is available from Appendix I, Worksheet XIII.

Using Students for Program Evaluation

Students constitute a useful resource for subjectively evaluating alternative education programs after more objective sources of data have been secured. Even though subjective evaluation is subject to bias and inconsistency, this type of evaluative data is useful because it results in feedback and suggestions from those individuals the program directly impacts. After all, the purpose of a school is to provide students with an education. What better source of evaluation is there for schools than the clientele receiving services, in this case an education?

This author has effectively used students for program evaluation in the

lab school setting. Annually, students are asked how the program bene-
fitted them and what they liked and disliked about it. Furthermore,
students are asked about the helpfulness of their teachers and other staff
members, the effectiveness of their methods and procedures, and what
changes they would like to see in the program. Staff members consider
the responses of students when undertaking improvement initiatives and
planning future programs.

A reproducible form for student evaluation of programs is available
from Appendix I, Worksheet XIV.

Using Staff for Program Evaluation

Staff members can be used for program evaluation in a manner similar
to that of students. Unlike demographic and collaborative team repre-
sentation, staff participation in the evaluation process is necessary because each member is directly involved in the program. Thus, both staff
members and students provide invaluable feedback and suggestions
drawn from personal experience instead of a checklist of compliance or
table of figures based on raw data or external observation.

This author has used both formal and informal means of securing staff
evaluation of programs. A series of open-ended questions have been used
in a structured response format for obtaining staff member input. On the
other hand, staff members have simply been asked to make a written
report evaluating the alternative education program, complete with recommendations and suggestions. A structured format of open-ended
questions seems to result in a broader, more comprehensive assessment
of the program from staff members. Instead of responding to only those
things that happen to come to mind, staff members provide open-ended
but guided responses to all areas of program operation.

EFFECTIVE PRACTICES IN STUDENT EVALUATION

Glasser (1992) contends that all teachers embrace the traditional
method of evaluating student progress, a method of evaluation that no
more than half of the students handle successfully. Glasser portrayed our
present method of evaluation in the following manner:

> I, the teacher will punish you unless you can show me on my, or our test
> that you know what I have just taught. If students do not succeed in

showing this to their teachers on a test that either the teacher or the school selects, they are punished with one or more of the following: given a low or failing grade, put in a low-track class, put in a special class, or eventually flunked. As these punishments pile up, which they do for well over half of the students, the punished students lack the strength to keep trying. (p. 236)

Quality schools evaluate based on all students doing competent work plus some work that is quality work. All students have a chance to learn without time constraints. Examples of alternative evaluation methods cited by Glasser involve no failure, self-paced learning, self-evaluation, striving for quality, demonstration of competence or mastery when ready, working together, getting credit for accomplishments, and getting an opportunity for improvement and grade enhancement.

In the spirit of Glasser's "competence plus quality" concept of evaluation, Figure 9.4 shows that formatively evaluating students based on 80% mastery of cognitive objectives determined from pretesting, and summatively evaluating students based on mastery gains determined after posttesting, are effective competency practices in alternative education. Additionally, formatively evaluating affective objectives through student portfolio development, and summatively evaluating students based on portfolio completion, are effective ways to evaluate both the quality and the quantity of work by students.

Initial Evaluation through Pretesting

Students enrolling in one of the alternative education programs com-

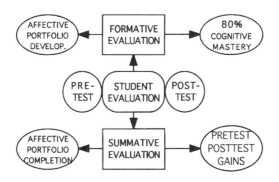

Figure 9.4 *Student evaluation.*

prising the lab school setting undergo an initial assessment of achievement by the school counselor. Learners are pretested using the Test of Adult Basic Education (TABE), a nationally normed test of achievement. Pretesting is initiated to determine student skill levels and appropriate placement in the curriculum. Learners receive individualized lesson plans tailored to their needs as a result of pretesting. The initial evaluation process positively impacts the meaningfulness of the formative and summative evaluation processes carried out subsequently to measure what has been learned in the areas of need identified through pretesting and lesson planning.

The Test of Adult Basic Education (TABE) is part of the prepackaged "Comprehensive Competencies Program" offered by the U.S. Basics Corporation.

Formative Evaluation

Hefner-Packer (1991) described formative evaluation as focusing on happenings throughout a program. Specifically, formative evaluation of students seeks to determine whether they are achieving their goals and following their prescribed plan throughout the school year. Formative evaluation can be achieved in many ways, but for our purposes, it is accomplished most effectively through ongoing cognitive mastery of content and affective portfolio development.

COGNITIVE MASTERY

One approach to individualizing instruction and improving learning, called "mastery learning," was developed by Benjamin Bloom, a noted educational psychologist, and his associates. Bloom's basic message is that even though differences in intelligence and aptitude do exist in every classroom, teachers can adjust the nature of instruction and the time allowed for each student so that more students can succeed (Ryan & Cooper, 1995).

Conceptual Background

Ryan and Cooper (1995) report that the effects of mastery learning strategies generally are favorable, particularly in connection with other instructional approaches, such as cooperative learning. The effectiveness of mastery learning is rooted in past problems concerning teaching and learning. Ryan and Cooper described the major problem researched by Bloom below:

> Most students are provided with the same instruction in terms of amount, quality, and time available for learning. When this occurs, students who possess more aptitude for given subjects will outperform students possessing less aptitude. But if one accepts that students are normally distributed according to aptitude, one can match the kind and quantity of instruction and the amount of time available for learning to the characteristics and needs of each student. Then the majority of students may be expected to achieve mastery of the subject, and hence the name "mastery learning." (p. 337)

The Concept in Practice

As a means of formatively evaluating student progress throughout the school year, this author set an objective mastery level of 80% for attainment of learning objectives by students in the lab school setting. The mastery level may vary due to the particular circumstances of a given program, but the same general principles apply. Students not reaching the objective mastery level after initial assessment are required to continue work on the objectives in question until mastery is attained. Students attaining lesson mastery, on the other hand, are allowed to move to the next lesson. The process repeats itself until unit mastery is attained, and eventually subject mastery becomes a consideration. Subject mastery is usually determined as part of a summative evaluation described in the following.

Through the individualization of instruction determined from pretesting and the use of self-paced, competency-based resources, mastery learning has become an effective practice in science, social studies, math, and English. Prepackaged programs are available that ascribe to the mastery learning principles. One such prepackaged program, consisting of a core curriculum of print material, reading supplements, computer-assisted instructional software, and videotapes in each subject, is available from the U.S. Basics Corporation in Alexandria, Virginia. This curriculum has been used effectively in the lab school setting by this author for the purposes of individualizing instruction and using mastery learning with alternative school students.

AFFECTIVE PORTFOLIO DEVELOPMENT

"Along with book bags and lunch boxes, many students now tote something new to school, portfolios of their work. The use of portfolios is becoming increasingly popular in U.S. schools as teachers look for alternatives to traditional tests to measure student progress" (Black, 1993, p. 44).

Conceptual Background

According to Black (1993), "portfolios are one answer in the search for alternative ways to assess students' performance . . . portfolios are supposed to show what students have learned and what their abilities are according to researchers Lorraine Valdez Pierce and J. Michael O'Malley". In her writings, Black provided selected research defining what is meant by portfolios:

> Judith Arter defines a portfolio as "a purposeful collection of student work that exhibits to the student and others effort, progress, or achievement in a given area or areas." F. Leon Paulson and Pearl R. Paulson emphasize process over product in their definition: "A portfolio is a carefully crafted portrait of what someone knows or can do." (p. 44)

Black contends that teachers might find someone else's definition of portfolios suitable, or they might choose to write their own. In any case, Black recommends that educators consider appropriate standards for judging portfolio materials, determining what should be included, and how to store portfolios, and communicating results to parents and policymakers. When planning to use portfolio assessments, educators can begin by considering the purpose, curriculum and instruction, content, assessment, management and logistics, and staff development. Teachers will need assistance throughout the process of portfolio assessment due to the difficult nature of its use.

The Concept in Practice

This author is using portfolio development in the lab school setting as a formative means of evaluating students in their affective education courses. Portfolio development is being used on a limited basis due to the problems that have been documented in the literature concerning reliability, standards, grading, and reporting. Many of these issues need to be resolved before portfolios can be effectively used across the curriculum.

Due to the nature of affective education, it seemed perfectly suited for portfolio development. Higher order thinking skills are often required when teaching morals, value, character, self-esteem, decision making, and problem solving—topics most often associated with affective education. Thus, portfolio development is the perfect method for providing students an opportunity for self-assessment, personal insight, and exploration. Students are able to use their creativity and self-expression to communicate what they have learned and how it applies to their lives.

Students in the lab school are required to develop a portfolio of personal journal writings, reports on issues affecting their lives, experiences in their service learning program, descriptive responses to questions concerning their identified risk areas, and assignments relating to specific areas of affective education. Students develop the portfolio throughout the semester, with evaluation occurring formatively during each of three grading periods.

Terminal Evaluation through Posttesting

During the course of instruction in the lab school setting, students are tested frequently to verify formative mastery of learning objectives designed as a result of pretesting. After course mastery has been declared through formative means of evaluation, final posttests are administered to determine benchmark gains in skill level. Posttesting in the lab school setting usually occurs at the conclusion of a semester or school year. An alternate form of the Test of Adult Basic Education (TABE) is administered to students and test results from both forms are compared.

Summative Evaluation

Hefner-Packer (1991) described summative evaluation as focusing on outcomes. "Summative evaluation weighs expected outcomes against actual outcomes. The primary question to be answered is, How much have students improved as a result of alternative education programs?" (p. 42). Hefner-Packer advocated summative reporting of evaluation findings to school or district staff so results can be used for decision making.

PRETEST/POSTTEST GAINS

After initial pretesting to determine skill level, formative evaluation of prescribed learning objectives, and terminal posttesting , summative comparisons are drawn to determine benchmark gains in skill level. Differences in pretest/posttest scores typically indicate grade level gains and/or the need for additional work at a particular skill level. These comparisons have been used in the lab school setting to determine grade level, promotion, course credits, and a return to regular school. More importantly, pretest/posttest comparisons generally indicate the effectiveness of our curriculum and our program in helping students.

PORTFOLIO COMPLETION

Summative evaluation, or more appropriately, "portfolio assessment" in affective education involves determining the degree of completion of a student's portfolio. In the lab school setting, formative evaluation of portfolios entails assessment of progress toward their development. Summative evaluation of portfolios, on the other hand, entails determining if students have completed the content requirements of the portfolio. Additionally, effort, progress, and insight are evaluated, as well as achievement. Instead of traditional grading methods (which is still one unsolved problem area in the world of portfolios), checklists and narratives are used to provide feedback and award credit. Teachers check for completion and provide comments on the various sections of the portfolio. Extra effort and creativity are considered when assigning grades or credit to portfolio completion.

REFERENCES

Berliner, D. C. 1984. "The half-full glass: A review of research on teaching," in *Using What We Know about Teaching,* P. L. Hosford (Ed.). Alexandria, VA: Association for Supervision and Curriculum Development, pp. 51–77.

Black, S. 1993. "Portfolio assessment," *The Executive Educator,* 2:44.

Brophy, J. 1982. "Effective teaching strategies for the inner city child," *Phi Delta Kappan,* 64:527–530.

Brophy, J. 1983. "Classroom organization and management," *The Elementary School Journal,* 83:265–284.

Burrello, L. C., & Sage, D. D. 1979. *Leadership and Change in Special Education.* Englewood Cliffs, NJ: Prentice-Hall, Inc.

Cummings, C. 1980. *Teaching Makes a Difference.* Smohomish, WA: Smohomish Publishing.

Georgia Department of Education. 1993. *Evaluation Manual.* Atlanta, GA: Georgia Teacher Evaluation Program.

Glasser, W., M.D. 1992. *The Quality School: Managing Students without Coercion.* New York: Harper Perennial Publishers, pp. 226–236.

Hawley, W. D., & Rosenholtz, S. J. 1984. "Good schools: What research says about improving student achievement," *Peabody Journal of Education,* 61:15–52.

Hefner-Packer, R. 1991. "Alternative education programs: A prescription for success," *Monographs in Education, Vol. 12,* C. T. Holmes (Ed.). Athens, GA: College of Education, University of Georgia, pp. 41–42.

Hunter, M. 1982. *Mastery Teaching.* El Segundo, CA: TIP Publications.

Kounin, J. S. 1970. *Discipline and Group Management in Classrooms.* New York: Holt, Rinehart and Winston.

Levin, T., & Long, R. 1981. *Effective Instruction.* Alexandria, VA: Association for Supervision and Curriculum Development.

Rinne, C. H. 1984. *Attention: The Fundamentals of Classroom Control.* Columbus, OH: Charles E. Merrill.

Rosenshine, B. 1983. "Teaching functions in instructional programs," *The Elementary School Journal,* 83:333–351.

Rosenshine, B., & Stevens, R. 1986. "Teaching functions," *Handbook of Research on Teaching.* New York: Macmillan Publishing Company.

Ryan, K. 1993. "Mining the values in the curriculum," *Educational Leadership,* 3(51):16–18.

Ryan, K., & Cooper, J. M. 1995. *Those Who Can Teach.* Boston, MA: Houghton Mifflin Co., p. 337.

Trohanis, P. L. 1985. "Designing a plan for in-service education," *Topics in Early Childhood Special Education,* 5(1):63–82.

SUGGESTED RESOURCES

U.S. Basics, "The Comprehensive Competencies Program," United States Basic Skills Investment Corporation, 1700 Diagonal Road, Suite 400, Alexandria, VA 22314.

Chapter 10

COMPLETING THE CYCLE

There is nothing permanent except change.

—Heraclitus

NEEDS ASSESSMENT: WHERE IT ALL BEGAN

When talking "program creation" with others, the same thought about needs assessments is expressed over and over again: "Dr. Chalker, I thought needs assessments were supposed to occur at the beginning of program planning, not after evaluation." In response, I affirm that needs assessment is used during planning for the purpose of developing a mission statement and goals and objectives during the process of creating alternative education programs. However, I am quick to add that ongoing needs assessment is critical to program improvement and expansion.

According to Swan (1990), the purpose of ongoing needs assessment is to develop priorities and goals for future program improvement based on problems, strengths, concerns, and other relevant factors such as rules, regulations, or other program requirements (Burrello & Sage, 1979; Trohanis, 1985). Swan went on to say that "the continuing emphasis on accountability and effectiveness has encouraged leaders to investigate program improvement on a periodic basis" (p. 1). According to Swan, needs assessments provide a valuable strategy for examining the quality of special programs, including alternative education programs.

USING EVALUATION AND ASSESSMENT OF NEEDS TO FACILITATE PROGRAM IMPROVEMENT

By beginning and ending program creation with needs assessment the alternative educator is able to see where the program is headed and where it has been. The assessment of needs after initial program evaluation indicates that the cycle of program creation is complete. At this point, program evaluation and assessment of needs should become a periodic practice as long as the program is in operation. This combination is the only effective means of determining the need for program improvement.

The results of program evaluation and ongoing needs assessment data can be effectively combined to facilitate program improvement. Those areas of the program found insufficient as a result of evaluation, combined with the determination of needs after assessment, can both contribute to program improvement. New components can be added to meet identified needs, others can be changed to reflect identified improvement variables.

USING EVALUATION AND ASSESSMENT OF NEEDS TO FACILITATE STAFF DEVELOPMENT

The results of both staff evaluation and terminal needs assessment can be used to facilitate staff development. Staff development based on both of these indicators strives to facilitate instructional improvement and support for students. For example, if the terminal needs assessment determines that support for dropouts is needed to slow a spiraling dropout rate, staff development can provide teachers with the tools to work with this segment of the population in the classroom.

Conceptual Background

"Teachers, administrators, and support staff need to receive preservice training that gives them the skills to create a school-relationship climate that promotes development and learning" (Comer, 1987, p. 14). With training in child development and behavior, Comer concluded that most teachers could help children at-risk close the developmental gap that prevents them from performing well. This training should give future educators opportunities to develop sensitivity, gain knowledge, and acquire skills in applying the principles of child development and behavior. He also postulated that preservice education should prepare future educators to work together with support staff.

Greene and Uroff (1989) described teacher training as consisting of instruction in learning styles, group process, communication skills, classroom management techniques, effective discipline methods, and problem-solving skills. They emphasized the importance of involving students in their own learning while building supportive relationships. This involvement strategy is an outcome of teacher training in the above skills (p. 80).

Maurer (1982) described the results of a thirty-hour intensive training program for teachers designed to assist with dropout prevention:

> At the end of the course, these teachers were significantly better able to incorporate into their classrooms those techniques of discipline, class-room management, and instruction that research has identified as effective in changing student performance. . . . Providing training to more than 50% of the teaching faculty meant that the project affected at least 90% of the students in the school. This training provided teachers with the necessary competencies to establish a therapeutic remedial academic program for a large number of disruptive potential dropouts. (p. 470)

Duke (1993) posited that "An on-site in service program that trains teachers on how to intervene early in the school year helps prevent many students from falling through the cracks" (p. 28). Duke contends that staff development enhances teacher efficacy by providing regular class-room teachers with a variety of interventions to assist at-risk students. In addition, it provides teachers and administrators a forum for openly discussing instructional issues in a positive manner. According to Barone (1989), an element crucial to teaching is the development of educational activities that can broaden students' horizons. Empowering teachers in this way includes the reeducation of teachers, the reduction of workloads, and the purchasing of material resources.

Cardenas and First (1985) advocated broadening the curriculum and teaching practices so that they better meet the needs of diverse student populations. Their recommendation is based upon the proposition that individual children have differing needs and abilities. Braddock and McPartland (1990) also advocated equipping teachers with useful teach-ing methods as a means of improving achievement. They found that cooperative learning, for example, a strategy that actively involves all students from a heterogeneous class in learning activities, is an effective way to improve achievement.

Hamby (1989) suggested providing staff development for all school personnel in the area of positive interpersonal relations and communication. This type of training helps teachers avoid adversarial situations between themselves and students. Different models of counseling and communication are used as instructional aids in this training (p. 24).

The Concept in Practice

Staff development in the lab school setting focuses primarily on issues related to at-risk students and how to better work with them. Staff evaluation occurring throughout the year, along with terminal needs assessment, contributed to the development of staff development activities conducted before the start of the new school year. Methods and strategies for working with alternative school students are based on documented deficiencies and needs from the evaluation and assessment process. As a result, entire programs are developed like the dropout program for helping staff members work better with students. During preplanning activities held the week before school starts, teachers receive a variety of staff development training topics relevant to the evaluation and needs assessment processes. This process prepares teachers to work with students in these areas needing improvement.

REFERENCES

Barone, T. 1989. "Ways of being at risk: The case of Billy Charles Barnett," *Phi Delta Kappan,* 71:147–151.

Braddock, H. J., & McPartland, J. M. 1990. "Alternatives to tracking," *Educational Leadership,* 47(7):76–79.

Cardenas, J., & First, J. M. 1985. "Children at risk," *Educational Leadership,* 43(1):4–8.

Comer, J. P. 1987. "New Haven's school-community connection," *Educational Leadership,* 44(6):13–16.

Duke, D. L. 1993. "How a staff development plan can rescue at-risk students," *Educational Leadership,* 50(4):28–33.

Greene, B., & Uroff, S. 1989. "Apollo High School: Achievement through self-esteem," *Educational Leadership,* 46(5):80–81.

Hamby, J. V. 1989. "How to get an 'A' on your dropout prevention report card," *Educational Leadership,* 46(5):21–28.

Maurer, R. E. 1982. "Dropout prevention: An intervention model for today's high schools," *Phi Delta Kappan,* 63(7):470–471.

Swan, W. W. 1990. "Needs assessments for special programs," *Monographs in Education, Vol. 11,* C. T. Holmes (Ed.). Athens, GA: College of Education.

Chapter 11

PERSPECTIVES IN ALTERNATIVE EDUCATION

Perspective is a certain point of view in understanding or judging things or happenings, especially one that shows them in their true relations to one another.

FUTURE IMPLICATIONS

For alternative education, the future has arrived! The field is growing so rapidly that it is history in the making. Even so, three practices have surfaced with implications for the future of alternative education. The first, programs for special education students, is controversial. The second, programs for elementary school students, has been rather slow to develop. Lastly, parental involvement, for decades has been a nightmare, a mystery unsolvable in many regular public schools. Addressing these areas may result in a more comprehensive playing field for alternative education.

What We Are Finding Out about Special Education Students

Despite the viewpoint of many special educators that the Individualized Education Plan (IEP) provides each special needs student with the appropriate modifications to a regular education, there is a place for alternative education in the schooling of these students. The IEP usually

161

addresses those factors attributed to the particular disability of the student in question. IEPs can only consider those attributes known to affect the student being served at any given time. Thus, it does not typically address factors attributed to the student's social maladjustment. Behviors attributed to the influence of peer pressure, low self-esteem, and dysfunctional family are not always symptomatic of the special education. student's particular disability. Drug and alcohol use, gang membership, carrying a weapon, disruptive behavior, rebelliousness, and criminal activity can affect any student regardless of level of functioning and type of disability. In the case of the special education student, many behaviors simply cannot be attributed to the identified disability.

The segment of the special education population that exhibits these types of behaviors requires assessment to determine the relationship between the observed behaviors and the disability in question. When IEP strategies and the efforts of the special education teacher become exhausted, school officials search, often unsuccessfully, for solutions to the problems being exhibited. With limitations in the number of suspension days allowed and interference with the stipulations of the IEP, administrators are limited in what they can do with the socially maladjusted, special education student. Without the appropriate, on-site special education teacher, alternative placement qualifies as one of these limitations.

Provisions for alternative placement for special education students require using a teacher with interrelated certification spanning grades K–12. The qualifications of such a teacher make it possible to serve students at all grade levels, with all types of disabilities in the school system. The most effective approach to providing these services when classes are self-contained is the Inclusion method of instruction. First, Inclusion does not require an additional classroom, because the Inclusion teacher provides instruction in the regular classroom setting, the least restrictive environment for special education students. Second, with inclusion, both regular and special education students can benefit because all students are to some degree at-risk, either academically, socially, or both. The Inclusion teacher and the regular classroom teacher join forces as a teaching team instead of working strictly with special education students on an individual basis. Instruction can be large-group focused or delivered to smaller groups, with each teacher assigned to a particular group for a specific instructional purpose.

What We Are Finding Out about Elementary Alternative Programs

The age at which children are characterized as at-risk continues to be lowered as the incidence of family dysfunction, poverty, drug abuse, and media exposure increases. Identification of students at-risk due to these types of circumstances presently occurs as early as kindergarten, and sometimes earlier. Students are acting out and exhibiting disruptive behaviors in the classroom at an equally young age. Such students are typically low achievers, resulting in grade retention at an early age. As a result, overage students are becoming more prevalent in the fourth and fifth grades. The characterization of overage students includes being labeled as displaced, a bully, disruptive to the educational process, and engaged in socially regressive behavior.

Ideally, alternative education will provide programs in the early grades as a proactive, preventive approach to later at-risk behavior. Intervention in the problems of multiple grade retention and the lack of achievement of students in the upper elementary grades needs to be addressed collaboratively with prevention efforts.

An effective practice for planning an initial alternative program for elementary school students is to start by serving kids with chronic problems. Once established, such a program can work toward expansion into prevention-based initiatives in the lower grades. For example, the program could be designed to accept students who are overage in the third, fourth, and fifth grades. Academic acceleration and/or behavior intervention for these disruptive students is an effective intervention method.

What We Are Finding Out about Parental Involvement

Many alternative educators are finding that gaining the involvement of parents is as difficult as it is for most regular public schools. Because alternative programs serve students who often have a history of unfavorable home and school circumstances, achieving parental involvement takes a great deal of effort, salesmanship, and patience on the part of alternative educators. Parents have often become alienated and disenchanted with the regular school experience, leading to apprehension when their children begin attending an alternative program. Another segment of parents spends the majority of their time working, acting as single parents, or are too consumed in family dysfunction to participate effectively in the alternative school.

Having parents applaud your efforts, progress, and triumphs while educating their children, often times a rare occurrence, does not qualify as parental participation. Parental participation means more. Much more.

After many disappointing and fruitless attempts at achieving maximum parental participation, the Institute of Effective Practices began to research the topic. What we found can be used as a foundation for alternative educators wanting to begin or improve a parental participation program. The following is a synopsis of our findings.

Cardenas and First (1985) promoted the removal of barriers to parental involvement accompanied by the creation of opportunities for parental participation. Parents may be given opportunities to participate in decisions about alternative school staffing, educational programming, school discipline, and resource allocation. "Future educators need to understand how to promote desirable home-school relationships so they can minimize the anxiety about school that undergirds parents' and students' distrust and alienation. Parents provide students with added resources and school people with added allies" (Comer, 1987, p. 14).

Hamby (1989) advocated the development of creative ways to take meetings to the parents if parents do not come to school for meetings, emphasizing that it is important to involve parents and students in deciding how this can be done (p. 22). Hamby also encouraged the involvement of parents in their children's learning, especially in the early grades. Classes for parents in how to help their children learn are also an important part of this process.

Maurer (1982) described a "Family intervention and parental training program with three purposes: family counseling, teaching parents more appropriate and effective discipline procedures, and mobilizing all the family resources to help students change" (p. 471). Maurer found that by training parents, changes taking place in the school were reinforced, parents were helped to deal more effectively with all of their children, and solid community support was garnered.

McLaughlin and Shields (1987) contended that parent involvement merits significant policy attention and public resources. Low-income and poorly educated parents want to play a role in their children's education, just as other parents do. In addition, a significant proportion of today's school children come from family situations that necessitate new ways to involve parents in their children's education. The development and support of effective parent-involvement strategies hinges on the attitudes and beliefs of the individuals involved (p. 158).

AFTERTHOUGHTS AND REFLECTIONS

An Honorable Profession

Alternative education is an honorable and rewarding field. Individuals and groups involved in alternative education or planning to do so will find that respect, gratitude, adoration, and admiration are just some of the feelings that are routinely expressed by students who cross their path. A former juvenile delinquent and troubled student put it best when he said to the program director, "Thanks for giving me the opportunity to come to your school and turn my life around. You deserve much respect!"

An Emotional Roller Coaster

Alternative education is also full of pitfalls, trials and tribulations, ups and downs, and mood swings! Stress, tension, and anxiety can dominate one's emotions if left unchecked. Therefore, it is imperative for alternative educators to develop a personal wellness program to neutralize stress and anxiety. Of course, having a sense of humor can help!

Alternative Educators as Modern-Day Heroes

Overworked and underpaid, alternative educators are routinely thought of as heroes and saviors by grateful students, parents, regular educators, caseworkers, and community leaders. Alternative educators rescue America's throwaways, those students who have fallen through the cracks or never fit in from the beginning. With the tremendous increase in the need for educational alternatives, this trend is expected to continue.

When You Know You Love It!

When being labeled a hero is just not enough and the roller coaster ride becomes too much, when you begin to wonder if you are at-risk because you feel overwhelmed with everything, just when these feelings begin to overcome you, it happens! Someone, somewhere, asks you what you do for a living. Whether in a plane, train, bus, car, or taxi, or at work, play, or school, it is always the same. You know you love the profession when you get on the proverbial soapbox and tell all. It could last hours or take a matter of minutes. It could be planned or spur-of-the-moment. Every bizzare incident, unusual circumstance, and hopeless situation turned good brings gasps and groans from admiring citizens. As you talk about your successes and failures, your gains and losses, and your triumphs and disappointments, you will find yourself beaming with pride, full of that fighting spirit, again. This reoccurring ritual simply reaffirms your dedication and reinforces your philosophy. It makes it possible for you to drag yourself out of bed each morning and return to school for another round of alternative education.

When You Know It's Working!

Every alternative educator has experienced the thrill of success, the joy of having a former student make it in the world. These are the types of experiences that keep the alternative educator "coming back for more." The following is a testimonial delivered by a former alternative education student who has done just that and more:

> My name is Larry Stigall. I am 18 years old and I was born in Wisconsin. My dad was in the military, so we were always on the move. My family was not rich, but I always had enough. My mother would punish me sometimes but my father's punishment would keep me on the straight and narrow. When I was fourteen years old, my parents divorced and I never know why. I was happy in the beginning because I had my way. I started coming in the house very late. My dad was not there, so I did it just because I could get away with it. It was hard for my mom to raise three kids, so I decided to take responsibility for myself but in a negative way. At age fourteen, I did not realize that my way was the wrong way. As a result of hanging on the streets, drinking became the cool thing to do. Drinking became a daily event because all my associates were doing it. I began doing silly things. I became violent, destructive, and very angry. For example, I can remember beating people up and throwing rocks at windows. I always felt like breaking things. At age sixteen, I started hanging out with drug dealers. I wanted to be cool and I wanted to be accepted, so I started selling drugs. I was so scared at first, but I earned a lot of money in very little time. I decided coming to school was a

waste of time when I could skip school and make even more money. I began carrying large amounts of cash and drugs around, causing my associates to give me a gun for protection. One day I decided to stay at school. I had the gun with me not knowing that I was about to get caught. Many teachers asked me about the gun, so I gave it up. Carrying a weapon to school is an automatic expulsion. My mother attended my disciplinary tribunal. School officials decided to give me a second chance by allowing me to go to the alternative school after the Christmas break. While hanging out with my friends over the holidays, they decided to hold up three boys. I did not realize what they were about to do until it was all over. My friends did not know that I knew the boys we were holding up. When the three boys filed the report, my name was the only name that was reported. I was picked up from my home and taken off to jail for two months. My short experience in jail was like an awakening to me. I realized that drugs, crime, and jail were not for me. Alternative school was exactly what I needed. The staff showed a great deal of concern for me. I could see that people were concerned and cared for me, but that they could only do so much. I knew that I had to be concerned about myself. The alternative school was responsible for my turnaround. I have also learned how to take something negative like anger and turn it into something positive like working with the handicapped. While attending the alternative school, I volunteered in their Service Learning Program. I am presently doing volunteer work at the Association of Retarded Citizens Thrift Shop. The alternative school helped me find a job at the local Food Lion grocery store. While working at the store, a young man asked me to visit his church with him. I now attend church every week, and enjoy going. I know that if I was going to succeed, I had to set a few short term goals. Graduation was a top priority. I began to spend time studying and getting extra help. My CVAE work study instructor taught me how to balance my time, and my grades immediately improved. Now that my grades were improving, I could also play basketball and track. Basketball was the one thing that I enjoyed doing, and I was very good at it. However, I could never play because of my grades. I am now proud to say that I am a member of the varsity basketball and track teams. My mother is also proud of me, but most importantly, I am proud of myself. I plan to graduate next year and attend a vo-tech school for construction. My long-term goals are to help my mother financially and to continue to be a positive role model for my younger sister.

Larry Stigall was recognized with his own day, May 16, 1995, at this author's alternative school. He is now a senior at the local high school and was recently recognized as "Most Improved Young Man" by the Vocational Opportunities Club of America. I had Larry speak to my classes in an effort to motivate and inspire students who are experiencing similar circumstances. The following correspondence is testimony that success may very well breed success:

Dear Dr. Chalker,

Since I first came to your school, I have enjoyed being a student in your program. I like this school more than any other school. I know some things I did at home, I now think back on. You make me understand some of the things I do are not worth the trouble doing. Some day, I wish I could do something like Larry did here at the school. But I see that it takes hard work. Well, I am going to cut this by saying thank you for being there for me when I did and did not need you. You are always here for me.

P.S. The most important thing I want you to do for me is to put me in my right grade. If that's okay, I will do what ever it takes to get there and get back in regular school.

Jermaine Powell

EPILOGUE

Policymakers could learn a few things about teaching, learning, and what students need by looking at what alternative education is doing with the so-called at-risk population. Individualized instruction, self-paced mastery learning, life skills courses, low pupil-staff ratio, enrichment opportunities, and flexible scheduling are just a few of the practices found effective with students in general.

Current school policy neither designs nor equips its schools with the resources to implement practices like those discussed here on a large scale. Schools are too large, pupil-staff ratios too high, traditions too strong, old habits too hard to break, and money too short for most regular schools to change the way they do things. Therefore, there will always be a need for educational alternatives to traditional schooling.

REFERENCES

Cardenas J., & First, J. M. 1985. "Children at risk," *Educational Leadership,* 43(1):4–8.

Comer, J. P. 1987. "New Haven's school-community connection," *Educational Leadership,* 44(6):13–16.

Hamby, J. V. 1989. "How to get an 'A' on your dropout prevention report card," *Educational Leadership,* 46(5):21–28.

Maurer, R. E. 1982. "Dropout prevention: An intervention model for today's high schools," *Phi Delta Kappan,* 63(7):470–471.

McLaughlin, M. W., & Shields, P. M. 1987. "Involving low-income parents in the schools: A role for policy?" *Phi Delta Kappan,* 69:156–160.

PLANNING COMMITTEE WORKSHEET

WORKSHEET I: CHOOSING A PLANNING COMMITTEE

Instructions:

1) Plan for a variety of different stakeholders representing a cross-section of the community.

2) Select individuals who are either knowledgeable about or have a vested interest in students at risk or alternative education.

3) Prime candidates for committee seats are community service providers and members of business and industry.

4) List your committe members in the appropriate category below.

SCHOOL SYSTEM REPRESENTATIVES
1) Teacher Representative: _____
2) Student Representative: _____
3) Parent Representative: _____
4) School Administrator: _____
COMMUNITY SERVICE REPRESENTATIVES
5) DFCS Representative: _____
6) Mental Health Representative: _____
7) Court Services Representative: _____
8) Public Health Representative: _____
BUSINESS/INDUSTRY/GOVERNMENT REPRESENTATIVES
9) Small Business Representative: _____
10) Industry Representative: _____
11) Public Official Representative: _____   (councilman, mayor, etc.)
12) Public Safety Representative: _____   (sheriff, police, state patrol)

Developed by Christopher Scott Chalker, (1995).

CONDUCTING A NEEDS ASSESSMENT

WORKSHEET II: EDUCATOR ASSESSMENT

Name _____   Position _____

School _____   Grades_____

1. How many of the students attending your school are not achieving a normal level of school success and educational attainment? _____

   List principle reasons for below average success:

2. In your particular school, how many students are in need of a non-traditional format, such as an accelerated program of instruction or individual makeup courses due to retention in grade? _____

3. Estimate the number of students who drop out of your school each year.
   _____

   List the principle reasons for dropping out:

4. What types of alternative education programs are needed to assist students at risk of dropping out due to the above reasons?

   List the types of programs needed:

Note: Adapted from Hefner-Packer (1991)

WORKSHEET III: COMMUNITY SERVICE ASSESSMENT

Name of Agency/Organization_____

Director_____   Phone_____

Please give the following questions your careful consideration. Place a ( ) check after the appropriate response(s) and include additional information.

1. Does your agency/organization provide DIRECT SERVICES to school-age youth? YES [ ]   NO [ ]   If YES, please check the appropriate age group(s):

   Under 16 years [ ]   16-18 years [ ]   Over 18 years [ ]

2. What type of DIRECT SERVICES do you provide the youth?

   _____ financial aid   _____ housing   _____ education

   _____ medical aid   _____ counseling   _____ employment

3. Does your agency/organization provide INDIRECT SERVICES to school age youth? YES [ ] NO [ ] If YES, explain briefly:_____
_____

4. In working with school-age youth, does your agency/organization:

   a. make school attendance a condition to services?   YES [ ] NO [ ]
   b. follow-up on school attendance?   YES [ ] NO [ ]
   c. assist students in determining educational goals? YES [ ] NO [ ]
   d. provide information regarding educational opportunities and
       options   YES [ ] NO [ ]

5. Does the local school district provide the educational options needed for your school-age clients? YES [ ]   NO [ ]

6. What additional options do you feel would be helpful? Explain briefly.
_____
_____

7. Approximately how many of your present school-age clients would benefit if an alternative education program were available? Estimate by age group.

   Under 16 years [ ]   16-18 years [ ]   Over 18 years [ ]

Note: From Hefner-Packer (1991).

WORKSHEET IV: CONSUMER ASSESSMENT

> The alternative school planning committee values your opinion concerning how well the school system meets the needs of at-risk children and families and the problems experienced in finding available educational alternatives.

1) What school system provided help do you and your children need most?

_____

_____

_____

2) What problems do you experience when you try to get school system help?

_____

_____

_____

3) Tell us about a good experience you have had with the school system?

_____

_____

_____

4) Tell us about a bad experience you have had with the school system?

_____

_____

_____

5) If you could change one thing about the present educational system, what would it be? _____

_____

_____

174

(continued from previous page)

Respond to the following by circling   yes or no.

6) Do you feel that children and families are educated on available educational services and the type of students these services effect?

YES   NO

7) Do you feel that the school system works cooperatively to ensure that the needs of all school children are met?

YES   NO

8) Do you feel that you need help in obtaining educational alternatives for your student aged child?

YES   NO

9) Do you feel that you need more school system assistance with your children and family in general?

YES   NO

10) Do you feel that the school system needs to provide alternative education programs for their students? If yes, what types of programs can you suggest?

YES   NO

_____

_____

_____

Additional   Comments:_____

_____

_____

_____

Developed by Christopher Scott Chalker, (1995).

175

WORKSHEET V: STUDENT DEMOGRAPHIC ASSESSMENT

1. How many students live in homes with one of the below arrangements?

    _____ foster parents _____ step-parents _____ single-parent _____ relative

2. By grade, how many students were retained last year:

    12th_____ 11th_____ 10th_____ 9th_____ 8th_____ 7th_____ 6th_____

3. By grade, how many students left school prematurely last year:

    12th_____ 11th_____ 10th_____ 9th_____ 8th_____ 7th_____ 6th_____

4. Of the above number, how many left school for the following reasons:

    Moved after requesting a transfer   _____

    Left without reason   _____

    Entered the job market or military   _____

    Suspended or expelled for disciplinary problems   _____

    Dropout   _____

    Referred to another educational program in the district   _____

5. Of the students who have been suspended, expelled, or dropped

    out of school in the past year, how many for the following reasons:

    _____Poor attendance   _____Apathetic, bored with school

    _____Chronic illness   _____Not accepted socially

    _____Behind in academics   _____Pregnancy / parenthood

    _____Drug abuse / alcoholism   _____Rebellion against school rules

    _____Peer Pressure   _____Family / personal problems

    _____Needed to help at home   _____Hostile, abusive behavior

    _____Need to work   _____Lack of options in school

6. Of the students who have left school in the past year:

    _____how many have returned to school

    _____how many have enrolled in a GED program

Adapted from Hefner-Packer, (1991).

MISSION STATEMENT WORKSHEET

WORKSHEET VI: DEVELOPING A MISSION STATEMENT

Developing a mission for the local school system's alternative education program:

Instructions:

1) Describe your vision for alternative education.

2) Describe your purpose for alternative education.

3) Discuss what the group's mission should be considering its vision and purpose.

What is your vision?

What is your purpose?

What is the group's mission based on its vision and purpose?

Developed by Christopher Scott Chalker, (1995).

GOALS AND OBJECTIVES WORKSHEET

WORKSHEET VII: DEVELOPING GOALS AND OBJECTIVES

Primary and Secondary Goals and Objectives

Instructions:

1) Describe your primary and secondary goals below.

2) List objectives designed to facilitate goal attainment.

3) List any questions, ideas, or concerns you have about the goals and objectives.

4) Consider whether these goals and objectives will change in the future.

5) Discuss your goals and objectives with the planning team and note areas of agreement and disagreement.

Primary Goal: 1) _____

Secondary Goals: 1) _____

2) _____

Objectives: 1) _____

2) _____

3) _____

Questions, Ideas, or Concerns: _____

Areas of Agreement: Areas of Disagreement:

Developed by Christopher Scott Chalker, (1995).

FACILITIES WORKSHEET

WORKSHEET VIII: FACILITIES PLANNING

Questions to answer:

Does your school system have sufficient existing classroom space available during the daytime for a school-within-a school program, if desired? If so, describe: _____

Does your school system have an existing classroom available during the daytime for use as an alternative classroom, if desired? If so, describe:

_____

What existing school facilities can be shared with a school continuation program held during the evening hours in the absence of sufficient daytime space?_____

Are there self-contained facilities available for a separate alternative program, if desired? If so, describe:_____

If available, are the facilities school system based or community based?

_____

The following resources and services linked to the availability of sufficient facilities are readily available for school-within-a-school, alternative classroom, and school continuation programs based in existing schools:	If considering a self-contained, separate alternative school, list below who will be responsible for furnishing the corresponding resources and services linked to the availability of facilities: "Key"
	1) Space available on-site
	1) Furnished by partner school
	2) Community based
	3) Furnished by business partner

(Continued on next page)

182

Preparation and/or transport of meals	[	]
Cafeteria	[	]
Physical education facilities	[	]
Media center/library	[	]
Classroom furnishings	[	]
Interagency services	[	]
Audio-visual equipment	[	]
Computer lab	[	]
Vocational facilities	[	]
Counseling and guidance services	[	]
Auditorium/Multipurpose room	[	]
Transportation	[	]
Other consideration	[	]
Other consideration	[	]

Developed by Christopher Scott Chalker, (1995).

183

BUDGETING WORKSHEET

WORKSHEET IX: BUDGET PLANNING

When budget planning for alternative education programs, use the spreadsheet below can be used to determine and enter proposed expenditures and the different sources of available revenue.

EXPENSES	SOURCES OF AVAILABLE REVENUE:					
	LOCAL	STATE	FEDERAL	PRIVATE	GRANT	SPONSOR
Teacher Salaries: [ ]						
Support Staff Salaries: [ ]						
Administrative Salaries: [ ]						
Fringe Benefits: [ ]						
Instructional Supplies: [ ]						
Office Supplies: [ ]						

(continued on next page)

185

EXPENSES	LOCAL	STATE	FEDERAL	PRIVATE	GRANT	SPONSOR
Curricular Materials: [ ]						
Equipment and Furniture: [ ]						
Renovations or building rent: [ ]						
Travel/Staff Development: [ ]						
Computers and software: [ ]						
Total Expenses						
Total Revenue: [ ]	[ ]	[ ]	[ ]	[ ]	[ ]

Subtract total revenues from total expenses: _____ - _____ = _____

Per Pupil Expenditures = _____

Developed by Christopher Scott Chalker, (1995).

ADAPTED TEACHER EVALUATION INSTRUMENT FOR ALTERNATIVE EDUCATORS—WORKSHEET X: FORMAL MODEL

ADAPTED TEACHER EVALUATION INSTRUMENT FOR ALTERNATIVE EDUCATORS USING NON-TRADITIONAL CLASSROOM METHODS AND PROCEDURES

Clarification:

This instrument is designed for school districts whos alternative programs are mandated to use a formal evaluation instrument but need an adapted model due to the non-traditional structure of their classrooms. Alternative programs using more traditional curricula, instructional methods, and classroom management procedures are encouraged to continue using their current instrument if satisfied with its program compatibility.

TEACHER_____   DATE:_____

SUBJECT(S) _____   GRADE LEVEL(S) _____

Evaluation Criteria: <u>S</u> = Satisfactory   <u>N</u> = Needs Improvement,

<u>U</u> = Unsatisfactory   <u>NO</u> = Not Observed

Score	AREA I: CURRICULUM AND INSTRUCTION

_____
A. Curriculum: Curricular content and level take into consideration each student's particular ability and needs.

Observations: _____

_____

_____

_____
B. Instruction: Instruction is individualized, self-paced, and student generated with or without teacher facilitation. A variety of instructional strategies are employed to facilitate instruction.

188

Instructional Observations (check all applicable):

STUDENT GENERATED INSTRUCTION

_____ With Facilitation   _____ Without Facilitation

___ Individualized	___ Individualized
___ Self-Paced	___ Self-Paced
___ Cooperative Groups	___ Independent Study
___ Role Playing/Modeling	___ Computer-Assisted
___ Interactive Learning	___ Peer Tutoring/Facilitation
___ Demonstrations/Aids	___ Teacher Inactivity
___ On-Task Facilitation	___ Testing Period

Did the focus more closely resemble traditional teacher generated instruction instead of the above choices?
Explain: _____

_____

Other Observations: _____

_____

_____   **C. Transfer of Learning:** The curricular materials and/or instructional methods provide for transfer of learning through linking content to relevant life experiences, to prior or future learning, or through associations.
Observations: _____

_____

Score	AREA II: STUDENT PROGRESS

_____   **A. Facilitating Engagement:** Engagement is facilitated either through the promotion of on-task behavior during classroom monitoring, through interactive learning using technology and multimedia, or through a variety of strategies, including cooperative group involvement, role playing, etc.
Observations: _____

_____

_____ **B. Monitoring Progress:** Student progress was monitored by interpreting either relevant student responses, contributions, performances, or products such as using assessment of mastery learning levels, portfolio development, personal interaction, contributions to cooperative learning groups, or graded work.

Observations: _____
_____
_____

_____ **C. Student Performance:** Students were provided reinforcement for adequate performances and feedback or correctives for inadequate performances.

___ **Adequate Performance**   ___ **Inadequate Performance**

___ Paraphrasing Response   ___ Providing Hints or Cues
___ Applying the Response   ___ Using Examples
___ Exending the Response   ___ Creating Smaller Steps
___ Connecting the Response   ___ Suggestions
___ Praising the Response   ___ Alternative Materials
___ Awarding the Response   ___ Encourage Repeat Attempt

Other Observations: _____
_____
_____

_____ **D. Supporting Students:** Support for students is conveyed through encouragement, lowering concern levels, dignifying responses, and by avoiding sarcasm, ridicule, and humiliating references.

Observations: _____
_____
_____

Score	AREA III: CLASSROOM MANAGEMENT

_____ **A. Organizational Structure:** Instructional time was optimized by strategies such as using efficient methods for transitions, materials distribution, and other routine matters, and by techniques that promote on-task behavior such as earned point systems, progressive level systems, or privileges awarded for productivity.

_____ **B. Physical Setting:** The physical setting allowed students to work without disruption, to obtain materials, and to move about easily. It also allowed the teacher to monitor the students and to move among them. Was the physical setting designed for both regular student seating and space for group counseling, cooperative groups, and technology and multimedia? _____ If not, what were the distinguishing characteristics of the classroom setting?

_____
_____
_____
_____

_____ **C. Behavior Management:** Appropriate behavior was maintained by monitoring the behavior of the entire class, providing feedback, and redirecting when necessary. Was on-task behavior optimized in an effort to minimize disruptive behavior in the classroom? _____ If not, make suggestions for improvement below:

_____
_____
_____
_____

Adapted from the Georgia Teacher Evaluation Program, Georgia Department of Education (1993).

ADAPTED TEACHER EVALUATION INSTRUMENT FOR ALTERNATIVE EDUCATORS—WORKSHEET XI: INFORMAL MODEL

INFORMAL TEACHER EVALUATION INSTRUMENT FOR ALTERNATIVE EDUCATORS USING NON-TRADITIONAL CLASSROOM METHODS AND PROCEDURES

Clarification:

This instrument is designed for alternative programs whos school districts have the flexibility to use an informal, unstructured evaluation instrument but need a version suitable for the non-traditional structure of their classrooms. Alternative programs using more traditional curricula, instructional methods, and classroom management procedures are encouraged to continue use of their current instrument if satisfied with its program compatibility.

TEACHER_____   DATE:_____
SUBJECT(S) _____ GRADE LEVEL(S) _____

Goal Statement (developed during goal setting phase):

Objective Statement (developed after goal setting):

Implementation Plan (curricular materials, instructional activities, student support, time frame, and student assessment):

(continued on next page)

Non-Instructional Duties:

Relationship with Parents/Colleagues:

Degree of Accomplishment (meets district standards, recommended areas of improvement, unsatisfactory areas):

Recommended Followup (activities, time frame for improvement):

Evaluatee Comments:

Summary Evaluation: _____ Satisfactory _____ Unsatisfactory:
_____ Continue with improvement plan _____ Dismissal

Evaluator's Signature	Date	Evaluatee's Signature	Date

Developed by Christopher Scott Chalker (1995).

PROGRAM EVALUATION
WORKSHEETS

WORKSHEET XII: DEMOGRAPHIC PROGRAM EVALUATION

Number of students served:_____   **Number of staff members:**_____

A) What was the number and percentage of parents attending each school related parent meetings during the course of the school year?

1. #_____ %_____   2. #_____ %_____   3. #_____ %_____

4. #_____ %_____   5. #_____ %_____   6. #_____ %_____

7. #_____ %_____   8. #_____ %_____   9. #_____ %_____

10. #_____ %_____   11. #_____ %_____   12. #_____ %_____

B) What was the number and percentage of students showing improvement in the basic skills according to a comparison of pre-test/post-test scores?

Reading: #____ %____   Writing: #____ %____   Math: #____ %____

C) What was the number and percentage of students promoted in grade?

#_____   %_____

D) What was the number and percentage of students successfully completing the alternative education program?   #_____   %_____

E) What was the number and percentage of students leaving the program for the following reasons?

Expulsion:	#_____	%_____
Dropout:	#_____	%_____
Adjudication:	#_____	%_____
Reintegration:	#_____	%_____
Move/Transfer:	#_____	%_____
Other reason:	#_____	%_____

(continued from previous page)

F) What was the number and percentage of students receiving job training and/or employment while in the alternative education program?

#_____   %_____

G) How many and what percentage of staff members beginning the school year, completed the year?   #_____   %_____

H) How many and what percentage of staff members completing the year received acceptable evaluations?   #_____   %_____

Developed by Christopher Scott Chalker (1995).

WORKSHEET XIII: PROGRAM EVALUATION BY THE COLLABORATIVE

Program administrators should be exposed to the below evaluation indicators early in the school year as a guide for program preparation. During actual evaluation, those indicators not applicable for existing programs should be marked as such using N/A. Applicable indicators should be marked as either *unaccomplished* or *insufficient* using the number "0" and *accomplished* or *sufficient* using the number "1". Comments can be recorded using the space provided after each indicator. After rating each indicator in a given category, the total number of points should be recorded in the blank to the right of the category title. After completion, the total number of points in the right hand column should be determined and divided by the total number of points possible to arrive at a percentage.

0 = Unaccomplished   1 = Accomplished   N/A   7 Points

PROGRAM PLANNING. . . . . ____

___ Established a Planning Committee_____

___ Assessed Needs_____

___ Developed a Mission Statement_____

___ Established Goals and Objectives _____

___ Planned for Facilities _____

___ Planned a Tentative Budget_____

___ Proposal for Program Approval_____

0 = Unaccomplished   1 = Accomplished   4 Points

PROGRAM DEVELOPMENT. . . . . ____

___ Collaborative Team Development_____

___ Staff and Human Resource Development_____

___ Material Resource Development _____

___ Funding Proposal Development _____

(continued on next page)

0 = Insufficient   1 = Sufficient   6 Points

PROGRAM IMPLEMENTATION: CURRICULAR PRACTICES. . . . . . ____

_ _ _ Basic Skills Education_____

_ _ _ Leisure Education_____

_ _ _ Life Skills Education_____

_ _ _ Affective Education_____

_ _ _ Career Education_____

_ _ _ Academic Enrichment_____

0 = Insufficient   1 = Sufficient   4 Points

PROGRAM IMPLEMENTATION: INSTRUCTIONAL PRACTICES. . . ____

_ _ _ Student Placement_____

_ _ _ Classroom Management_____

_ _ _ Teaching and Learning_____

_ _ _ Student Evaluation_____

0 = Insufficient   1 = Sufficient   6 Points

PROGRAM IMPLEMENTATION: STUDENT SERVICES. . . . . ____

_ _ _ School-to-Work Transition _____

_ _ _ Service Learning_____

_ _ _ Guidance and Counseling_____

_ _ _ Student Recognition_____

_ _ _ Business and Community Partnerships_____

_ _ _ Interventions for Chronically Disruptive Students_____

(continued on next page)

199

0 = Insufficient   1 = Sufficient   6 Points

PROGRAM EVALUATION. . . . . _____

___ Staff   Evaluation_____

___ Program   Evaluation_____

___ Student   Evaluation_____

___ Summative   Needs   Assessment_____

___ Using Evaluation and Assessment of Needs_____
to Facilitate Program Improvement

___Using Evaluation and Assessment of Needs_____
to Facilitate Staff Development

TOTAL POSSIBLE: 33

TOTAL SCORED: _____

PERCENTAGE: _____

WORKSHEET IXV: PROGRAM EVALUATION BY STUDENTS

In the space provided below, express your opinions, concerns, or any other thoughts you may have concerning the alternative education program by circling the desired response or writing out your own answers.

1) Effectiveness of the program so far on you:

        a. very effective

        b. somewhat effective

        c. not very effective

2) What's your opinion of the staff? _____

_____

3) Have you or will you benefit from this experience?

        a. Yes

        b. No

        c. Somewhat or maybe (circle one)

      Explain your answer _____

_____

4) Explain in detail some things that you like about alternative education?

_____

_____

_____

_____

5) What are some things that you disliked about alternative education?

_____

_____

_____

_____

(Continued from previous page)

6) Do you think staff members were helpful?   **Yes**   **No**   Please explain.

_____

7) What was your favorite way of being taught while in alternative

education?   _____

_____

8) What was your favorite subject?_____Why? ____

_____

9) What are some changes you would like to see made in alternative

education to make it more effective for students and teachers?

_____

_____

_____

_____

10) Use the space below and the back of this page to express any other

thoughts you may have about your alternative education experience or any

related matters.

_____

_____

_____

_____

_____

_____

_____

_____

_____

Adapted from Short (1988).

The Advantage Press, Inc. 1988. *Discipline Advantage Learning Packet System.* Lisle, IL: Author.

Agency for Instructional Technology. 1994. *Workplace Readiness: Education for Employment.* Bloomington, IN: AIT.

Barone, T. 1989. "Ways of being at risk: The case of Billy Charles Barnett," *Phi Delta Kappan,* 71:147–151.

Barry, B.W. 1986. *Strategic Planning Workbook for Nonprofit Organizations.* St. Paul, MN: Amherst H. Wilder Foundation.

Bearden, L. J., Spencer, W. A., & Moracco, J. C. 1989. "A study of high school dropouts," *The School Counselor,* 37(2):111–119.

Beck, M. S. 1991. "Increasing school completion: Strategies that work," *Monographs in Education, Vol. 13,* C. T. Holmes (Ed.). Athens, GA: College of Education, University of Georgia.

Berliner, D. C. 1984. "The half-full glass: A review of research on teaching," in *Using What We Know about Teaching,* P. L. Hosford (Ed.). Alexandria, VA: Association for Supervision and Curriculum Development, pp. 51–77.

Bialo, E. R., & Sivin, J. P. 1989. "Computers and at-risk youth: A partial solution to a complex problem," *Classroom Computer Learning,* 19(5):35–39.

Black, S. 1993. "Portfolio assessment," *The Executive Educator,* 2:44.

Boyce, K., & Cairn, R. W. 1991. "Orientation and training," *The Generator,* 11(3):6.

Boyer, E. L. 1987. "Early schooling and the nation's future," *Educational Leadership,* 44(6):4–6.

Braddock, H. J., & McPartland, J. M. 1990. "Alternatives to tracking," *Educational Leadership,* 47(7):76–79.

Bronfenbrenner, U. 1986. "Alienation and the four worlds of childhood," *Phi Delta Kappan* (February):430–436.

Brophy, J. 1982. "Effective teaching strategies for the inner city child," *Phi Delta Kappan,* 64:527–530.

Brophy, J. 1983. "Classroom organization and management," *The Elementary School Journal,* 83:265–284.

Bucci, J. A., & Reitzammer, A. F. 1992. "Teachers make the critical difference in dropout prevention," *The Educational Forum,* 57:63–69.

Burrello, L. C., & Sage, D. D. 1979. *Leadership and Change in Special Education.* Englewood Cliffs, NJ: Prentice-Hall, Inc.

Cardenas J., & First, J. M. 1985. "Children at risk," *Educational Leadership,* 43(1):4–8.

Chalker, C. S. 1994. "A Description of Separate Secondary Alternative School Programs in Georgia in 1993–94," unpublished doctoral dissertation, The University of Georgia, Athens, GA.

Clough, G. 1990. "Student assistance program screening: Matching needs with resources," *Adolescent Counselor,* 42(4):38–39, 53.

Comer, J. P. 1987. "New Haven's school-community connection," *Educational Leadership,* 44(6):13–16.

Conrad, D., & Hedin, D. 1987. *Youth Service: A Guidebook for Developing and Operating Effective Programs.* Washington, DC: Independent Sector.

Conrad, D., & Hedin, D. 1991. School-based community service: What we know from research and theory," *Phi Delta Kappan,* 72(10):743–749.

Corey, G. 1977. *Theory and Practice of Counseling and Psychotherapy.* Monterey, CA: Brooks/Cole.

Correct Quotes. 1991. Novato, CA: Wordstar International Incorporated.

Cuban, L. 1989. "At-risk students: What teachers and principals can do," *Educational Leadership,* 46(5):29–32.

Dearman, N. B., & Plisko, V. W. 1979. *The Condition of Education* (Publication No. ADM 82-921). Washington, DC: U.S. Government Printing Office.

Dinkmeyer, D. C., Pew, W. L., & Dinkmeyer, D. C., Jr. 1979. *Adlerian Counseling and Psychotherapy.* Monterey, CA: Brooks/Cole, p. 311.

Dreikurs, R. 1968. *Psychology in the Classroom.* New York: Harper & Row.

Duckenfield, M., & Swanson, L. 1992. *Service Learning: Meeting the Needs of Youth at Risk.* Clemson, SC: National Dropout Prevention Center.

Duke, D. L. 1993. "How a staff development plan can rescue at-risk students," *Educational Leadership,* 50(4):28–33.

Edgar, S. 1989. "An analysis of the effects of an intervention program on academic, social, and personal adjustment of at-risk and retained seventh and eighth grade students" (doctoral dissertation, Northern Arizona University, 1987), *Dissertation Abstracts International,* 49:7920A.

Emmerich, M. 1983. "Training tomorrow's leaders today," *Educational Leadership,* 40(6):64–65.

Fizzell, B. 1990. Personal communication via letter. Edu-Serve, Vancouver, WA 98685.

Frank, C. 1984. "Equity for all students: The New York City promotional gates program," *Educational Leadership,* 41(8):62–65.

Frymier, J. 1989. *A Study of Students at Risk: Collaborating to Do Research.* Bloomington, IN: Phi Delta Kappa Educational Foundation.

Frymier, J., & Gansneder, B. 1989. "The Phi Delta Kappa study of students at risk," *Phi Delta Kappan,* 71:142–146.

George, P., & Mooney, P. 1986. "The Miami Boys Club delinquency prevention program," *Educational Leadership,* 43(4):76–78.

Georgia Department of Education. 1993. *Evaluation Manual.* Atlanta, GA: Georgia Teacher Evaluation Program.

Georgia Department of Education. 1994. *Crossroads Interim/Annual Report.* Atlanta, GA: Division of Research, Evaluation and Assessment.

Georgia Department of Education. 1995. *Workplace Readiness: Education for Employment.* Bloomington, IN: Agency for Instructional Technology.

Gibson, R. L., & Mitchell, M. H. 1986. *Introduction to Counseling and Guidance.* New York: Macmillan Publishing Company.

Glasser, W. 1984. "Reality therapy," in *Current Psychotherapies* (3rd ed.), R. J. Corsini (Ed.). Itasca, IL: F. E. Peacock, pp. 320–353.

Glasser, W., M.D. 1986. *Control Theory in the Classroom.* New York: Harper and Row, Publishers, pp. 7–16.

Glasser, W., M.D. 1992. *The Quality School: Managing Students without Coercion.* New York: Harper Perennial Publishers, pp. 226–236.

Greene, B., & Uroff, S. 1989. "Apollo High School: Achievement through self-esteem," *Educational Leadership,* 46(5):80–81.

Gross, B. 1989. "Can computer-assisted instruction solve the dropout problem?" *Educational Leadership,* 46(5):49–51.

Guralnik, D. B. 1992. *Webster's New World Dictionary of the American Language,* 2nd ed. Simon and Schuster, Publishers.

Hahn, A. 1987. "Reaching out to America's dropouts: What to do?" *Phi Delta Kappan,* 69:256–263.

Hamby, J. V. 1989. "How to get an 'A' on your dropout prevention report card," *Educational Leadership,* 46(5):21–28.

Hancock, V. E. 1993. "The at-risk student," *Educational Leadership,* 50(4):84–85.

Harris, J., Hedman, C., & Horning, M. 1983. "Success with high school dropouts," *Educational Leadership,* 40(6):35–36.

Hawley, W. D., & Rosenholtz, S. J. 1984. "Good schools: What research says about improving student achievement," *Peabody Journal of Education,* 61:15–52.

Hefner-Packer, R. 1991. "Alternative education programs: A prescription for success," *Monographs in Education, Vol. 12,* C. T. Holmes (Ed.). Athens, GA: College of Education, University of Georgia.

Holland, J. L. 1985. *Making Vocational Choices: A Theory of Vocational Personalities and Work Environments.* Englewood Cliff, NJ: Prentice Hall.

Holmes, C. T., & Matthews, K. M. 1984. "The effects of nonpromotion on elementary and junior high school pupils: A meta-analysis," *Review of Educational Research,* 54(2):225–236.

Hunter, M. 1982. *Mastery Teaching.* El Segundo, CA: TIP Publications.

Iowa Association of Alternative Schools. 1990. Brochure. Available from Kathy Knudtson, 1212 7th St. S.E., Cedar Rapids, IA 52401.

Isaacson, L. E. 1985. *Basics of Career Counseling.* Boston, MA: Allyn & Bacon, Inc.

Jenkins, J. R., & Jenkins, L. M. 1987. "Making peer tutoring work," *Educational Leadership,* 44(6):64–68.

Kaufman, R. A. 1972. *Educational System Planning.* Englewood Cliffs, NJ: Educational Technology Publications, Inc.

Keefe, J. W. 1986. "Advisement programs: Improving teacher-student relationships, school climate," *NASSP Bulletin,* 69(489):85–89.

Kenney, A. M. 1987. "Teen pregnancy: An issue for schools," *Phi Delta Kappan,* 68:728–736.

Klausmeier, H. J., & Weber, L. J. 1984. "Improving secondary education in Wisconsin," *Educational Leadership,* 41(6):80–84.

Kounin, J. S. 1970. *Discipline and Group Management in Classrooms.* New York: Holt, Rinehart and Winston.

Lehr, J. B., & Harris, H. W. 1988. *At-Risk, Low Achieving Students in the Classroom,* 1st ed. Washington, DC: National Education Association.

Levin, T., & Long, R. 1981. *Effective Instruction.* Alexandria, VA: Association for Supervision and Curriculum Development.

Mackey, J., & Appleman, D. 1983. "The growth of adolescent apathy," *Educational Leadership,* 40(6):30–33.

Maryland Student Service Alliance. 1989a. *Courage to Care, the Strength to Serve: Reflections on Community Service.* Annapolis, MD: CZM Press.

Maryland Student Service Alliance. 1989b. *Draft Instructional Framework in Community Service.* Baltimore: Maryland State Department of Education.

Maurer, R. E. 1982. "Dropout prevention: An intervention model for today's high schools," *Phi Delta Kappan,* 63(7):470–471.

McLaughlin, T. F., & Vacha, E. F. 1992. "School programs for at-risk children and youth: A review," *Education and Treatment of Children,* 15(3):255–267.

Mitchell, S. T., & Johnson, P. H. 1986. "Richmond's response to students at risk," *Educational Leadership,* 43(5):62–64.

Morley, R. E. 1991. *Alternative Education.* Clemson, SC: Clemson University, National Dropout Prevention Center.

National Assessment of Educational Progress. 1985. "The reading report card: Progress toward excellence in our schools; trends in reading over four national assessments 1971–1984," Princeton, NJ: National Assessment of Educational Progress.

National Crime Prevention Council. 1988. *Reaching Out: School-Based Community Service Programs.* Washington, DC: Author.

Natriello, G., McDill, E. L., & Pallas, A. M. 1985. "School reform and potential dropouts," *Educational Leadership,* 43(1):11–13.

Ogden, E. H., & Germinario, V. 1988. *The At-Risk Student: Answers for Educators.* Lancaster, PA: Technomic Publishing Company, Inc.

Orr, T. M. 1987. *Keeping Students in School.* San Francisco, CA: Jossey-Bass Publishers.

Pellicano, R. R. 1987. "At-risk: A view of social advantage," *Educational Leadership,* 44(6):47–49.

Peng, S. 1983. *High School Dropouts: Descriptive Information from High School and Beyond.* Washington, DC: National Center for Education Statistics, U.S. Department of Education.

Pogrow, S. 1990. "Socratic approach to using computers with at-risk students," *Educational Leadership,* 47(5):61–66.

Ramirez, A. 1990. "These are the hallmarks of effective dropout programs," *The Executive Educator,* 12:23–25.

Raywid, M. A. 1994. "Alternative schools: The state of the art," *Educational Leadership,* 52(1):26–30.

Richardson, V., Casanova, U., Placier, P., & Guilfoyle, K. 1989. *School Children At-Risk.* New York: The Falmer Press.

Rinne, C. H. 1984. *Attention: The Fundamentals of Classroom Control.* Columbus, OH: Charles E. Merrill.

Rosenshine, B. 1983. "Teaching functions in instructional programs," *The Elementary School Journal,* 83:333–351.

Rosenshine, B., & Stevens, R. 1986. "Teaching functions," *Handbook of Research on Teaching.* New York: Macmillan Publishing Company.

Ryan, K., & Cooper, J. M. 1995. *Those Who Can Teach.* Boston, MA: Houghton Mifflin Co., pp. 130–137.

Ryan, K., & Cooper, J. M. 1995. *Kaleido Scope: Readings in Education.* Boston, MA: Houghton Mifflin Co., pp. 271–278.

Sagor, R. 1993. *At-Risk Students: Reaching and Teaching Them.* New York: Watersun Publishing Company.

Scardamaglia, R. 1993. "Teachers as student advocates," *Educational Leadership,* 50(4):31.

Short, P. M. 1988. "Planning and developing in-school suspension programs," *Monographs in Education,* Vol. 9, C. T. Holmes (Ed.). Athens, GA: College of Education, University of Georgia.

Slavin, R. E., Karweit, N. L., & Madden, N. A. 1989. *Effective Programs for Students at Risk.* Needham Heights, MA: Allyn & Bacon.

Smink, J. 1990. *Mentoring Programs for At-Risk Youth.* Clemson, SC: Clemson University, National Dropout Prevention Center.

Swan, W. W. 1990. "Needs assessments for special programs," *Monographs in Education, Vol. 11,* C. T. Holmes (Ed.). Athens, GA: College of Education, University of Georgia.

Trohanis, P. L. 1985. "Designing a plan for in-service education," *Topics in Early Childhood Special Education,* 5(1):63–82.

United States Department of Labor. 1994–1995. *Occupational Outlook Handbook.* Washington, DC: U.S. Government Printing Office.

Wager, B. R. 1993. "No more suspension: Creating a shared ethical culture," *Educational Leadership,* 50(4):34–37.

Walls, M. W. 1990. "The promise of a job keeps dropout-prone kids in school," *The Executive Educator,* 12(4):22–23.

Wehlage, G. G., Rutter, R. A., & Turnbaugh, A. 1987. "A program model for at-risk high school students," *Educational Leadership,* 44(6):70–73.

Wehlage, G. G., Rutter, R. A., Smith, G. A., Lesko, N., & Fernandez, R. R. 1989. *Reducing the Risk: Schools as Communities of Support.* New York: The Falmer Press.

Yaffe, E. 1982. "More sacred than motherhood," *Phi Delta Kappan,* 63:123–130.

York, P., York, D., & Wachtel, T. 1982. *TOUGHLOVE.* New York: Bantam Books, pp. 149–169.

Young, T. 1990. *Public Alternative Education.* New York: Teachers College Press.

Christopher Scott Chalker, a researcher, practitioner, and author in the field of alternative education, began his career in Liberty County, Georgia, in 1982 as a physical education and health teacher. In 1987, Dr. Chalker worked as a high school counselor for one year before taking a position as assistant principal at the same school. In 1991, due to an intense desire to make more of a personal impact on the lives of at-risk youth, Dr. Chalker answered the call to start an alternative program from scratch. Four years later, Dr. Chalker still heads the now fledgling L.E.A.D. Program (Liberty Educational Alternatives Division). He looks forward to a lifelong career providing educational alternatives to disadvantaged, dislocated, and at-risk youth and adults.

Dr. Chalker received his bachelor's degree from Western Michigan University, his master's and specialist degrees from Georgia Southern University, and his doctorate from the University of Georgia. He is certified in the fields of educational administration, school counseling, pupil/personnel services, and physical education and health. In addition, Dr. Chalker is a state-certified probation officer working part-time as a federally funded In-School Probation Officer. His dissertation research consisted of a study of alternative education for at-risk youth. Dr. Chalker has published several journal articles in this field prior to his current work.

Dr. Chalker presents his work on alternative education nationally. Interested parties can reach Dr. Chalker by writing: The Institute of Effective Practices in Alternative Education, Alternative Education Presentations Unlimited, P.O. Box 2297, Hinesville, Georgia 31310. To speak to Dr. Chalker or inquire about an updated address, call 912-876-3795.